Born and brought up in the north of England, Richard Fenning spent 14 years as CEO of Control Risks, the global consultancy that specialises in helping businesses out of tight spots in difficult countries. He now works as a leadership coach and is a regular media commentator on world affairs. He lives in Sussex.

'A fascinating insight into the space where politics and business meet, filled with wit and wisdom. Highly recommended'
Lord Sedwill, former UK Cabinet Secretary and National Security Adviser

'A must-read for every student of geopolitics, amateur or academic, professional or private. This beautifully written memoir is much more than that: a roller-coaster ride of risk, full of insights and implied advice, more relevant than ever in today's uncertain world. Richard's sense of humour, and of irony, and his golden pen, make even the most appalling experiences enjoyable. Strongly recommended'
Sir Sherard Cowper-Coles, former British Ambassador to Israel, Saudi Arabia and Afghanistan

'Take a spoonful of Evelyn Waugh, add a sprinkle of P.J. O'Rourke and garnish with a touch of Michael Palin. Fenning is not just wry, perceptive and informative: he is also laugh-out-loud funny, way more often than any CEO has a right to be'
Boris Starling, author of The Official History of Britain

D1502854

WHAT ON EARTH CAN GO WRONG

Tales from the Risk Business

Richard Fenning

EYE BOOKS
NON-FICTION

Published by Eye Books
29A Barrow Street
Much Wenlock
Shropshire
TF13 6EN

www.eye-books.com

First edition 2021
Copyright © Richard Fenning 2021

Cover design by Nell Wood
Typeset in Times New Roman

British Library Cataloguing in Publication Data
A catalogue record for this book is available from the British Library

ISBN 9781785632242

For
Rhoda and Leo
who gave me roots and wings

Ozymandias

I met a traveller from an antique land,
Who said— 'Two vast and trunkless legs of stone
Stand in the desert... Near them, on the sand,
Half sunk a shattered visage lies, whose frown,
And wrinkled lip, and sneer of cold command,
Tell that its sculptor well those passions read
Which yet survive, stamped on these lifeless things,
The hand that mocked them, and the heart that fed;
And on the pedestal, these words appear:
'My name is Ozymandias, King of Kings;
Look on my Works, ye Mighty, and despair!'
Nothing beside remains. Round the decay
Of that colossal Wreck, boundless and bare
The lone and level sands stretch far away.
Percy Bysshe Shelley

Contents

Foreword

IT IS ONE O'CLOCK in the morning in Tripoli. I am sharing a bed with a colleague. We are bedfellows out of logistical necessity rather than carnal choice. He is lying next to me wearing nothing but a pair of skimpy green underpants. He is deeply and blissfully fast asleep, and snoring like Darth Vader eating broken glass. Outside, there is the near-constant sound of automatic machine-gun fire – the deadly, metallic *tack-tack-tack* of AK47s being fired with reckless abandon. Through the window I can see the night sky illuminated with terrible beauty by tracer rounds. Inside, the toilet in the bathroom is malfunctioning, flushing loudly and constantly. I am wide awake, edgy and nervous, sweating in the hot North African night. Listening to this extraordinary orchestral ensemble, a bizarre combination of the banal and the ballistic, I think to myself: how in the world did I get to be here?

The reason was that I spent nearly thirty years consuming a daily diet of kidnappings, terrorist attacks, coups d'état, massive frauds, corruption scandals, cyber-attacks, data breaches, earthquakes, hurricanes, pandemics and, in the case of Libya, promising revolutions that went horribly wrong. After a while, you start to think that this is all that happens in the world, that all we ever do is lurch from one major crisis to another. If your time is spent guiding people away from the rocks or helping rescue survivors, then you tend to see calm seas and sunny skies merely as the lull between storms.

My job was to help international companies stay safe, to peer around the corner and warn them of trouble ahead. When that was not possible or there was no room to dodge out of the way, then it was time to help them to gird their loins, stiffen their sinews, weather the storm and deploy all manner of mixed metaphors to keep the ship afloat and the show on the road.

For nearly three decades, I was on the move, living and working all around the world. I became adept at turning up somewhere strange, trying to figure out what had gone wrong, dispense some kind of solution and move on. It was a contrasting combination of feeling both energised and exhausted at the same time. Pepped up by the exhilaration and the challenge but drained by the jet lag and the tedium of near-constant travel.

It was an odd life on the frazzled edge of globalisation. I was a member of a peculiar species of weirdly evolved primates: laptop warriors who live their life in airplanes, airports and soulless beige hotels, for whom the notion of a work-life balance is an odd antiquated concept. Work was a way of living not just a way to earn your living, a notion largely unknown to previous generations of executives who were mostly spared the tyranny of twenty-four-hour global connectivity.

I have recorded here some of my observations, both of the many strange situations I found myself embroiled in and also my recollections of some of the places that I got to know. These range from the exotic to the familiar, from places you may choose for a family vacation to those that you probably never want to visit if you can possibly avoid it. Many will be familiar territory to travellers and tourists; others are more off the beaten track.

This is a book about a nearly three-decade journey into the deep recesses of the risk and security industry. Along the way, we will meet some strange folks in the backstreets of Rio and Delhi, some oddballs in Bogotá and Baghdad, be unnerved in Moscow and Nairobi, get lost in Lagos, become befuddled in Tokyo and Shanghai and stumped in Washington DC. We will see what happens when innocent people find themselves very much in the wrong place at the wrong time. But if you tire of the geo-drama and fancy having your prurience tickled, we will also have a close encounter with a retired porn star, hear a cautionary tale about the devastating consequences of toxic flatulence and have an uncomfortable brush with a penis enlargement operation that went sadly wrong.

This is not a book about greatness and heroism, nor is it a book about despair and dystopia. It is about setting forth and, on the way, becoming a tiny bit braver. It is about learning – through trial and error – to distinguish what to be scared of and what not. It is also a tale of becoming less sure, more uncertain and replacing simplicity with complexity, the paradox of learning more but understanding less. Or if that sounds a bit dispiriting and nihilistic, then it is about how the baffling kaleidoscope of humanity never fails to surprise and upend our preconceived notions of the world in ways that can frustrate, confound and delight us in equal measure.

I hope you may be occasionally intrigued, perhaps have some of your views challenged and hopefully, at times, be amused. In places my misgivings about Britain's historical self-image will come to the fore, yet I have unfathomable reserves of affection for and pride in the country that moulded me and set me loose in the world. I hope that comes through.

My travels took me around the world on an annual repetitive loop. I met politicians of honest good-standing, others of dubious repute and some who should not be allowed to use scissors unsupervised. I encountered business leaders of the highest calibre and others of eye-watering incompetence. And given the nature of the work, I also had my fair share of brushes with the shadowy demi-monde of espionage and intrigue. Many of these people I liked enormously. Some gave me the creeps. And others scared the living daylights out of me.

I have had a few encounters worthy of some gratuitous name-dropping, including a very grumpy Margaret Thatcher at a drinks party in Tokyo. She had just taken part in a live television debate with the Japanese prime minister during which the cameras had started rolling before she was ready. The Japanese viewing public had seen her snapping at the poor sound engineer who was trying to adjust her earpiece while she was taking off her earrings. She had shooed him away like a naughty spaniel.

'Prime Minister, I think it gave people the chance to see your human side', I offered, trying to be helpful. She stared back at me, puzzled. She had understood each word I had said but had never heard them all in the same sentence before. 'Yes', she suddenly announced, wagging her index finger at me, 'my human side, my human side'. She turned to her pugnacious press secretary, Bernard Ingham, and told him to write that down in his notebook.

That evening, Mrs. Thatcher was distracted, tired and

seemingly diminished as she tried unsuccessfully to stop her stiletto heels from sinking into the soft grass on the embassy lawn. Henry Kissinger, by contrast, was anything other than diminished when I met him a few years later in New York. It was raw power with a hint of menace. Bill Clinton, meanwhile, was spellbinding. All folksy phraseology and quicksilver intellect.

Mostly my world has been about trying to tip the scales for people who are not rich and famous, enabling them to be safe and successful where otherwise they may have been defeated. It has been a privilege to have followed in the shadow of some remarkable colleagues. Men and women better able than I to absorb other people's stress and anxiety and help them navigate to safety across treacherous terrain.

I am a regular kind of person who has had the good luck to do an unusual job. A job that changed me. Not in any profound, fundamental sense – a Yorkshire childhood and a Methodist education took care of the hard-wiring – but in ways that only now am I able to slowly discern. There has been the occasional brush with danger. I say that from the perspective of someone with a low threshold for risk. Faced with obvious peril, my instincts are to scarper quickly in the opposite direction. The primeval software that our early hominid ancestors relied on to prompt them to leg it back to the cave when they encountered a sabretooth tiger in the woods, is for me still in tip-top condition.

The chapters that follow start by looking at how the risk business has grown and developed over time. There are then ten chapters looking at specific countries, each of which illustrates something of the world I have got to know over the past thirty years. The book concludes with chapters on the nature of risk, including a look at how we have been facing the COVID-19 pandemic, and then a view on how risk and danger affects each of us individually.

I have tried my best to be fair, conscious that there are very few absolutely bad people and a similarly small number of the truly heroic. In places, my impartiality gives way to polemic. I make no apology for that. This is my personal response to the bizarre world I have experienced. The opinions are all mine and I take full responsibility for all the errors, of both fact and judgement. And while I have grown muddled and bewildered by what goes on out there and sceptical and cynical about power and those who wield it, I hope my faith in humanity and my optimism about the future are still alive and kicking.

1

Stepping out of the shadows

I The age of exploration

THE MODERN RISK BUSINESS is widely regarded as starting in the early 1970s. Firms like Kroll Associates in New York and Control Risks in London, providing security and investigative advice to other businesses, were an entrepreneurial response to specific high-profile problems that were increasingly besetting ambitious global companies. Stolen money that needed tracking down across multiple jurisdictions or kidnapped executives languishing far from home in need of rescue – these were some of the headline-grabbing issues that needed fixing. In part, they were a private sector response to a public sector capability-deficit, as national governments faced constraints on the assistance that they could or were willing to offer to multinational companies keen to spread their global wings.

To be fair, this was less of a brand-new invention and more of a reimagining. Pinkerton detectives had been available for hire since Scotsman Allan Pinkerton set up shop in Chicago in 1850. Indeed, the origins of deploying the right kind of specialised talent to figure out how to get one step ahead of the competition, stay safe and sort out nasty situations goes back much further.

In fact, you could say it all began with Sir Francis Drake. When Queen Elizabeth I found herself heavily in debt, her country isolated by hostile European powers and her subjects riven by the religious turmoil wrought on them by her father's break with Rome, she had an idea. She would invest in an emerging market fund.

She would not have used this kind of terminology. But that, in effect, was what she did. She needed to make some speculative high-risk investments. She staked most of what she had on the possibility of massive returns. Returns that would reflate the exchequer, allow her to build up the naval resources to deter the prospect of invasion and also distract her spiritually distressed people with a big wallop of jingoistic pride. It turned out to be a master stroke. And the man she called on to execute this bold plan was a little-known sea captain from Devon called Francis Drake.

At the time, Drake had grown bored of maritime life in England. He was in West Africa trying to muscle in on the Spanish monopoly in transporting African slaves across the Atlantic to the new Spanish territories in the Caribbean. On one of these voyages to the New World, Drake had started attacking the newly established Spanish ports in what we now call Panama. He would steal anything worth stealing, ransom off the wealthy merchants and then burn the place down before the Spanish navy had a chance to intervene and chop his head off. He started to get rich and came to the notice of the Spanish, who understandably loathed and feared *El Draque*, offering a reward of what would now be about $8 million for his capture or death. He had also come to the attention of the Queen and her chief spymaster, Sir Thomas Walsingham.

Had Drake been born a few hundred years later, he would have made a superb hedge-fund manager. He could spot an opportunity where others saw only risks, he could execute a plan quickly, discreetly and efficiently and he had a knack for persuading otherwise cautious people to back his incautious schemes. He also had an almost insatiable taste for adventure, was mostly devoid of any kind of moral conscience and was recklessly criminal. In short, he was just the man for the job.

Elizabeth, a canny judge of the male ego if ever there was one, decided to harness Drake's formidable capabilities. She turned him from pirate to privateer. She backed his voyages both financially and officially and would later have him knighted. But he had to up his game. It was no longer sufficient just to be an irritant in Spain's imperial side. He had to start the wholesale looting of the gargantuan amounts of gold and silver that Spain was systematically stealing and shipping back to Europe from Peru and Chile.

Drake was wildly successful. He accumulated a personal fortune and returned even greater sums to his investors, particularly his royal patron, the Queen. He also found fame as an explorer by becoming only the second person to circumnavigate the earth. And he became a national hero when he defeated the Spanish Armada – the fleet that the now totally exasperated Spanish king, Philip II, had dispatched to invade England.

He never lived long enough to enjoy the life of the modern master of the universe. He did not have the chance for a Damascene conversion and become the billionaire philanthropist dedicated to eradicating the very same vices that had made him rich in the first place. He never got to posture pretentiously at the Tudor equivalent of the World Economic Forum in Davos, wear tight-fitting pantaloons designed for a man half his age or indulge in nauseating egomania with the top lute-playing musicians of the day. He died of dysentery back in Panama, aged 55.

Drake's status as one of Britain's great national heroes is fragile. His involvement with the slave trade and his piratical ways do not stand up to modern, more enlightened scrutiny. But he started something. Drake understood that his success was dependent on three things: good intelligence, the right security and a cool calibration of the risks, enabling him to generate high returns in volatile parts of the world. This spirit, rather than the grim operational reality, continues to provide the inspiration for many people to opt for a life in the world of modern-day business risk. In pure, unmodified form, it is also responsible for the persistence of mercenary activity beyond the pale of acceptable commercial or moral behaviour. Yet that core, original spirit of adventure and calculated risk-taking, repurposed and adapted for contemporary ethical norms, is what still attracts large numbers of people to seek a professional path with more sizzle and spice than other more conventional career options.

Of course, the less savoury aspects of how Britain became the economic and political superpower it once was have long-since been glossed over. Where they have broken cover and blundered out into the open recently, they have been caught in the controversial, often toxic quagmire of historical moral relativity in which one person's intrepid national hero is another person's exploitative trader in human misery. Drake was both. Nevertheless, warts and all, one strand of Britain's national story is dominated by that original Tudor innovation of seeking commercial advantage amid geo-political volatility.

The modern international company is no longer the extension of a single country's prestige in corporate form that it once was. Instead, big businesses have tried to become stateless, globalised, shape-shifting entities floating on oceans of tradeable data, seeking arbitrage advantage between different parts of the world which they define as markets not as nation states. Modern politicians, eager for the sugar rush of cheap populism and pushing more nationalist agendas, may try to lasso them back into line and get them to pay more tax. But in the main, they have slipped the leash.

By the end of the Seventies, the risk business, this new version of an old industry, was up and running, just as the world was enjoying a significant uptick in international trade. Indeed, the world was about to change in ways that nobody could really anticipate as ambitious but often ill-prepared companies ventured into new and unfamiliar markets. New markets brought new problems.

By then, the era of the amoral merchant adventurer running amok at the intersection of red-blooded capitalism, espionage and other people's politics was mostly over. While these new companies may have been able to trace their inspirational lineage back to the likes of Drake, they now had to play by a different set of rules. Business ethics had not yet become the obsession it is now, and corporate social responsibility was pre-embryonic. It was still a corporate sperm swimming around in the dark, looking for a socially responsible egg emitting a weak beacon of receptivity. But the rules of the game were changing. Big companies were coming under greater scrutiny and could no longer afford to act as if they had undergone an ethical lobotomy.

So too the risk industry. The stage was set for the arrival of a new type of company. A type that operated not beyond the pale but within the law and the boundaries of decent corporate behaviour. It was time to step out of the shadows. In those early days, governments were often suspicious and disapproving of the private sector poking around in the world of security and intelligence. As a fresh-faced newcomer, I once found myself attending a meeting at the British Foreign and Commonwealth Office. We were shown into a splendid wood-panelled room to be met by an up-and-coming diplomatic grandee with an illustrious family lineage. 'Ah, here come the princes of darkness,' he announced, with maximum condescension. It seemed a little unkind as we were there– pro bono – to help him resolve an embarrassing and delicate situation involving a British citizen in South America. Years later, the same now fully-fledged grandee welcomed me to his palatial ambassadorial residence with much warmer words and copious quantities of whisky and soda.

After these early teething troubles, it became clear that sustainability meant no longer emulating Tudor adventurers but acting lawfully and in ways that did not draw the ire of governments and regulators around the world. My great friend Simon Adamsdale and the late Arish Turle from Control Risks spent several months in a Colombian jail in 1976 after being arrested while successfully negotiating the release of a kidnapped American business executive in Bogotá. Their incarceration was eventually deemed illegal and they were released and pardoned. But there is nothing like a stint in Bogotá's notorious La Modelo prison to give you the chance to realise that if this business is going to prosper, it needs some guard rails.

This was the decisive step, even if some of the early pioneers still had a whiff of roguish glamour about them. Many of them continued to carry a little dust on their boots and feel the siren's lure of exotic exploits in obscure locations. Even now not everybody is on best behaviour all of the time. Every few years, some throwback to an earlier swashbuckling dogs-of-war, guns-for-hire era will emerge to grab the international headlines with some nefarious *Boys' Own* tale straight from the pages of a John le Carré novel. There are still plenty of very rich people in the world who feel that the normal rules do not apply to them. When it comes to securing rare-earth minerals in Africa or avoiding judicial process in Japan, they want direct access to the particular sets of skills that the former intelligence and special forces community has to offer and, in some quarters, is still ready to supply – for a price.

There was no need to fly below the radar. There was enough perfectly legitimate business to be had, not least because at the end of the Eighties the world changed dramatically in favour of the risk business. Indeed, the industry has a lot to thank Mikhail Gorbachev and Deng Xiaoping for in triggering the start of a multi-decade boom. The Cold War had just come to an end and history was, according to one over-quoted American political scientist, apparently a thing of the past. The Soviet Union had abruptly dissolved and been replaced by a free-for-all brand of casino capitalism. China meanwhile had made the more orderly decision to switch to its version of market economics after the massed anti-government protests in Tiananmen Square in Beijing had jolted the Chinese authorities onto the path of economic reform.

Suddenly a whole chunk of the world that had previously

been off-limits to business was now hungry for investment and expertise. There was lots of work to be had helping new investors understand the changing political dynamics behind these new opportunities, figuring out who they were likely doing business with, what hidden liabilities lurked in the shadows of opaque markets and making sure they stayed safe in unfamiliar territory. All of this gave the risk industry the air in its wings to grow and expand.

Elsewhere in the world, change was afoot with international trade organisations being beefed up. In April 1993, just as I was starting in the industry, NAFTA was ratified by the US Congress and the Maastricht Treaty creating the European Union came into force in November. Five months later the World Trade Organisation was created. We didn't realise it at the time, but we were entering the era of globalisation, that epoch when barriers to trade started to fall, new rules were written and virtually the whole of the world was open for business. Suddenly it seemed everybody was going everywhere, and global growth exploded. Deep in the thick of it, it was hard to comprehend quite what revolutionary forces were at work reshaping the global economy so radically.

This sense of infinite possibility in a world in which capital flowed freely across borders in search of hitherto unimagined opportunities also led to outbreaks of massive over-exuberance and grandiosity. One of my stranger encounters was with a mergers and acquisitions lawyer who walked into my office in London claiming to represent the interests of a Middle East investment fund with royal connections. He was fluent and self-confident, with an overly firm handshake. He was wearing an almost very well-cut suit – apart from his trousers. They were several inches too short, as if he was expecting the Thames Barrier to give way at any moment.

I now know always to be suspicious of men with too-short trousers.

He had a lot to say. Just occasionally he would stop talking long enough to allow me to speak. When he did it was clear, though, that he was not listening. He was just pausing to reload. Soon he was off again on another round of bankers' bingo. This is a common game in the City of London, Wall Street and wherever else money mingles with privilege and entitlement. He reeled out the names of a dizzying but predictable array of private schools, universities, regiments, banks, brokerage houses, friends and colleagues. It was the usual suspects and you mentally tick them off on an imaginary bingo sheet as he tries to impress you. Before I got to a full house, he realised that he was wasting his time with me and he got to the point.

On behalf of his client, he explained, he would like to buy Zimbabwe. I raised my eyebrows as he outlined some hair-brained agricultural production scheme that would provide food security for the Middle East and economic rejuvenation for Zimbabwe. He hoped that I would help in persuading then-President Mugabe to accept some substantial financial inducement to hand over the reins of power and retire, even richer than he already was, to Malaysia. As I had never met Robert Mugabe, had never been to Zimbabwe and was not in the habit of bribing heads of state, I suspect I was not the first person he had approached with his daft idea. I declined the opportunity, and he was off in search of the next sucker. He was playing the percentages game: ask enough people and someone will agree to help with your nutty plan. Eventually, he went to jail. It took a while, and a manhunt across several continents with the help of Interpol, but he got his just deserts eventually.

All of that was in the future when I started in the industry in 1993. My interview at Control Risks was a strange affair. Three former British army officers asked me a series of near-impossible to answer questions. While I was floundering around trying to craft a response, they set about answering their own questions for me. I was basically a bystander at my own interview. Eventually, I picked up the courage to enquire, somewhat tentatively, what it was exactly that they wanted me to do. It was clear that this was the first time they had given this subject any material consideration and they looked mildly irritated that I had asked such a specific question. They paused, furrowed their brows and then ignored me and continued answering each other's questions. I left the room bemused but intrigued.

In the coming decades, business would boom. The world would become safer, healthier and more prosperous than at almost any time since we first dragged ourselves from the primordial sludge. From the early 1990s, the global economy would quadruple in size over the next thirty years, a billion people would be lifted out of poverty, access to sanitation and medicine would expand exponentially and child mortality would halve. And it seemed that the threat of nuclear self-destruction had receded. It was, by almost any measure, a period of extraordinary material progress.

But all these grand statistics did not translate into a sense of universal wellbeing. Partly, it was the uneven geographical distribution of the fruits of economic expansion. You were certainly likely to be much better off if you were Chinese rather than Congolese during this period, from Manhattan not Michigan, Belgravia not Bolton. And you were better placed if you were setting off to work each morning clutching your laptop and smartphone rather than as a manual worker clinging to the wreckage of a declining industrial heritage. But it was about more than geographical chance. Aggregated data showing we are safer does not make us feel secure. Impressive progress in economic expansion does not translate into a general sense of prosperity. Feeling insecure and fearful or confident and relaxed is not the consequence of a logical formula. It defies the simple calculus of cause and effect.

II   The unholy trinity: war, terror and hubris

In retrospect, the clues were there that this brave new world of globalisation contained the seeds of its own comeuppance. There were certainly early indicators that it was not all going to be a bed of roses. Just as I was starting work at Control Risks in 1993, a young Kuwaiti-born Pakistani national called Ramzi Yousef attempted to blow up the World Trade Centre in New York. His plan was to detonate a massive car bomb in the underground parking bay below the north tower. The intention was to cause this tower to collapse and bring down the south tower as well. The plot failed but it was a terrible harbinger of what would occur eight years later on 9/11 when the same target was attacked but this time using hijacked planes as the delivery mechanism. And it seemed to be a family business. Ramzi Yousef's uncle turned out to be

Khalid Sheikh Mohammed, named as the principal architect of the attacks by the 9/11 Commission report.

Like millions of other people, I watched in horror as the 9/11 attacks unfolded on television. I was in London having just returned from many years living in New York. I headed back there on the first flight from London once air travel was deemed safe to resume, a desperately sombre journey, sitting on the airplane among grieving relatives. Arriving in Manhattan, the air was thick with dust from the collapsed towers and the city smelt of what it was, a still-smouldering acrid bonfire. Ahead, were weeks of scrambling to help companies suddenly shocked by their own sense of vulnerability to put in place – *post facto* – the mechanisms to keep their businesses and people safer in a new, more vulnerable world. This is a business that often echoes to the sound of stable doors being bolted. But in those first few days in New York, I was struck by the extraordinary resilience and defiance of New Yorkers. I realised emphatically that however appalling and shocking terrorism can be, it is an unequal battle when confronted by ordinary people who collectively refuse to be cowed.

9/11 set in chain the wars in Afghanistan and Iraq that would take so many lives, cost trillions and prove more enduring and harder to conclude than even the most stony-faced pessimists felt at the time they kicked off. They also unleashed a virulent destabilising virus in the Middle East. It would lay the foundations for the ill-fated Arab Spring and its terrible backlash in Syria and elsewhere. It would sharpen the wealth and opportunity disparity that fuels so much resentment and upend the power dynamics of an always volatile region. And it would act as an accelerant to the growth and spread of the mutating nightmare of radical Islamic terrorism.

The aftermath of the wars in Iraq and Afghanistan was a

game-changing moment for the risk business. Removing the Taliban in Afghanistan and Saddam Hussein and the Baathists in Iraq proved relatively simple given the overwhelming firepower and military expertise that America and her allies were able to bring to bear. But both countries quickly fell into states of chronic insecurity and the vast numbers of Western diplomats, aid workers, economic advisers and consultants that descended on Kabul and Baghdad needed to be kept safe. Later, in 2008, the international oil industry would arrive in Iraq and they too would find that revitalising the country's oil wealth carried a big security bill. Step forward the international risk and private security industry.

In the absence of an effective Iraqi or Afghan police force and with no trusted local security industry, there were enormous opportunities for those of us willing and able to plug the security gap left by the decapitation of the regimes. It became a feeding frenzy, swelling the coffers of many established firms but also attracting a host of newcomers racing to stake their claim in what they thought, with some justification, was going to be a new gold rush. As we shall see in a later chapter, this stampede became notorious for attracting more than its fair share of undesirables, some of whom behaved shamefully. On a less newsworthy level, it also taught the industry vital lessons about how to operate in countries that have functioned on the brink of failure for decades, riddled with corruption, sectarianism, poverty and endemic violence.

I became a CEO in the middle of this maelstrom. It was like holding a tiger by its tail. The world seemed to be in flux and opportunities and challenges for the business and the industry were all-consuming. I was learning how to lead while struggling to stand upright in the wind tunnel. On my first morning in the job, I was given a book about what new CEOs should do in their first hundred days. It contained the usual guff about setting a vision, declaring intent and marking your arrival by announcing some high-profile departures from the senior management team – the so-called 'swinging corpse' strategy. The same day, a colleague, Ali, was murdered by a sectarian mob in Baghdad. It took his sons five days to find his body in one of the city's many overflowing morgues. I checked the index of the book; there was nothing that seemed particularly relevant.

It was not just turmoil in the Middle East that led to a huge growth in demand. The surge in oil prices from the late 1990s encouraged many international oil companies to seek new opportunities in remote and inhospitable places, thereby making themselves a target for all kinds of terrorists, insurgents and malcontents. More business needed more people. The risk industry requires people with all kinds of contrasting skills and backgrounds. Unsafe frontier markets require resourceful men and women who enjoy life on the edge. Clients operating in the remotest and most inhospitable corners of the planet rely on their unflappable qualities to organise their security, fix their problems and, if it all gets too tricky, to get them out of there as quickly as possible.

The military can be a good training ground for this type of work. So too is working in a refugee camp, delivering aid, being a foreign correspondent, a spy and, believe it or not, being a schoolteacher. You also have political analysts with extraordinary academic credentials able to elucidate the way in which the macro-drama of global geopolitics has a direct impact on individual companies, particularly those making big bets in odd places. In the most extreme of locations, you will want to turn to the former special forces folk whose usually quiet demeanour, modest reticence and far-away stare tell of horrors seen and heroics untold. It is tempting to ask them to share some of the details from their more hair-raising exploits, many of which have captured the public's imagination over the years. Most are extremely reluctant to tell you anything. By and large, the old adage holds true: if they talk about it too much, they were not actually there.

Complex crises often require complex people. The ability to sit with a distressed client for weeks, months, sometimes years, requires considerable reservoirs of stamina and resilience. You also need lateral agility. Risk takes many forms: terrorists and criminals, fraudsters and hackers, bad politics and worse economics, scary weather and mutant viruses. What is consistent is the ability to be with people facing an existential threat to their business and often the wellbeing of their people. I have seen tough executives actually shake with fear – and for good reason – when they realise, they have inadvertently incurred the wrath of a Colombian cartel, a Russian mafia group, or, indeed, a Canadian Hells Angels gang. It does not need to be an exotic geography to be scary. I have seen similar acute anxiety in Montreal, Liverpool and Sydney.

You need to be able to act as a lightning rod for other people's chronic anxiety. You need to exhibit empathy, steadfastness and trust. You should also have something of the ardent birdwatcher about you: the ability to be well-positioned, constantly alert and observant, looking for barely perceptible changes in behaviour. The industry breeds peculiar people with some unusual quirks to their personalities. Out in the field, they need to display qualities of endless patience and tolerance. They must completely sublimate their own egos to keep their clients focused and sustained through the darkest and longest of times. Back in the office, everything changes. The calmest of individuals become querulous, low egos become prima donnas and the easiest-going and most adaptable of companions become psychotically pernickety pedants.

Managing all of these different types of people across multiple nationalities and cultures can test the patience of a saint. There are moments when you could not feel prouder, when you are left in open-mouthed awe at the ingenuity, integrity and bravery of selfless people pushing themselves to the limit for each other and their clients. Years' later, I still feel goosebumps thinking of colleagues and friends who have stood firm and protected clients besieged by armed mobs in Iraq, pulled bodies from fatal plane crashes, searched for dead relatives in the aftermath of tsunamis and hurricanes and held out for weeks in Ebola-ravaged parts of West Africa, waiting for help to arrive. Then there are other moments. Moments when the same people have driven you to the edge of sanity. When you collapse to the floor in frustration and curl up in the corner, foetus-like, sobbing for your mother.

It was not all about war and terrorism. In 2008, the world economy was taken to the brink by a financial elite seemingly impervious to their responsibilities and apparently exempt from bearing subsequent responsibility. Financial instruments had been designed to trade mind-warpingly large sums of money by programming computers to do things that hardly anybody (nobody) could really understand. We had fallen into the trap of thinking we are much smarter than we really are. The brains we use to devise all this financial complexity have used the same operating system and have had the same cognitive capacity for millennia. The brain that developed hundreds of thousands of years ago to pick berries and track deer is essentially the same brain that nowadays enjoys lying on the sofa, eating crisps and watching wrestling. No wonder we fucked it all up.

The complex circuitry of global capital markets was seen as the arterial life-support mechanism for a growing world economy. As the global financial crisis unfolded, it seemed to be its key vulnerability, particularly when poor people's debts were packaged up and used for a game of electronic pass-the-parcel, with disastrous consequences when the music stopped. Even before the crisis, there were plenty of people who felt that the ever more complex world of finance and big business provided too much scope for unbridled greed and financial skulduggery. Every few years, the headlines would be grabbed by wrongdoing on a grotesque scale. In the 1990s, the energy-trading company Enron came crashing down, causing untold collateral damage. In the Noughties, we were shocked by the breathtaking scale of Bernie Madoff's trickery in New York. More recently, the complicity of people who should know much *much* better in Malaysia's gigantic 1MDB scandal or the Wirecard collapse in Germany is hard to forgive. Add it all up and you have the ingredients for a big shift in public trust.

These were crimes committed and enabled by the already rich, sometimes famous and very often insufferably self-satisfied, drenched in the heavy cologne of hubris. They involved sums of money so far beyond the comprehension of normal people that you get some sense of why so many now feel that capitalism is like a rigged card game. Is it any longer the most effective means of harnessing the self-interest of the individual for the collective benefit of all?

This combination of over-engineered financial markets, spectacular corporate failures and the perennial ingenuity of fraudsters has been an ore-rich seam for other parts of the risk business. Over the past thirty years, regulators and governments have been engaged in a corporate governance arms race. As every new outrage or systemic failure occurs, they ratchet up the rules and regulations only for some new, apparently unforeseeable catastrophe to occur that leaves regulators with egg on their face. Each time there is a brief moment of soul-baring, of public penance and the paying of fines. But then the hubris kicks back in before any proper atonement or catharsis can occur, and the cycle continues.

It will be ever thus. There are parts of the financial services industry where there is just so much money to be had, and where people of modest ability can become rich beyond their wildest dreams. With these vast fortunes to be made, it is just too tempting and too easy to take a moral holiday and subvert the rules. Most bankers understand their responsibilities not to break the system that delivers so much. But small numbers of rogue traders, crafty fraudsters or the serially incompetent, lurking within highly leveraged banks, can cause carnage on a wholly disproportionate scale. Not surprising then that spectacular crashes occur that leave us teetering on an economic cliff-edge. Dangerously excessive risk is baked into the system.

As may be obvious by now, the scandal-prone proclivities of the financial services industry bring out my inner Methodist. I am conscious that I sound very puritanical. And hypocritical. I have been the massive beneficiary of the persistent recidivism of people working within a financial system where the built-in propensity for things to go wrong on a huge scale almost guarantees a steady stream of work for the risk industry. Forensic accountants, data analysts and financial investigators are ready to pick through the aftermath of an endless stream of collapses, outrages and lawsuits. In between times, they can turn their hand to helping with the ever-increasing burden of often hastily cobbled together regulatory compliance that valiant regulators attempt to retrofit into the industry. Many of these cases are on a massive, multi-jurisdictional scale and are mind-numbingly complex. They can keep the investigative community busy for years.

These too are people of particular talent and often quirky personality. You have former law-enforcement officers, lawyers and accountants who have escaped the normal claustrophobic confines of their profession and who now spend all day, every day forensically investigating other people's wrongdoing. They live so deep in a world of fraud, corruption, money laundering and criminal malfeasance that they become profoundly cynical about the very basic concept of human decency. If you offer them a pay rise or a promotion, they look at you with pathological distrust, wondering what the catch is. They see laptops, phones, computers not as the now commonplace accoutrements of the modern workplace but as the repositories of incriminating evidence to demonstrate yet again the baseness and venality of human beings.

I had a client who had enjoyed a career at the very top of the FBI. He had retired from the government and gone to work for a large Wall Street bank. His mandate was to try to keep them on the straight-and-narrow after another big blot on their copybook had – to everyone's shock and horror – landed them in the soup. He was miserable. One afternoon we sat putting the world to rights in his small office in the World Trade Centre, a few weeks before it was attacked. He explained how he had gone from a job defending the nation to one that entailed ensuring that nothing very bad (such as jail time) happened to executives young enough to be his children who could earn more in an afternoon that he had in a lifetime of exemplary government service. It was an uneven struggle. He left shortly afterwards, just before 9/11, and spent his days fly-fishing instead.

III   The empire bytes back

Before we all throw in the towel and head off to an Alpine euthanasia clinic, it is worth pausing to remember that it has not just been a tale of violence, greed and vengeance. Away from the geo-political psychodrama and corrupting greed, technology has opened up extraordinary new economic vistas. 1993 also heralded possibly the most profound change of our age, even if few of us spotted it at the time. CERN, the nuclear research facility in Switzerland, released its world wide web software, making it free for public use. Just to nail my colours to the mast: in the unlikely event that I had invented the basic software for the internet, I would not have given it away gratis. No way: I would have fully embraced the life of a decadent monopolist reaping in the billions until the end of time.

But this was an act of civic generosity that helped transform the nature of work, upended orthodox business models and altered our daily lives in ways that have left us reeling with the psychological torque brought on by such sudden change.

And we can only assume that the pace of this change is set to increase further as quantum computing, artificial intelligence and goodness knows what else hurtle towards us. As this revolution unfolds, it will untether the power of datasets so big that we cannot be sure our weedy homo sapiens brains will manage to keep up.

Technology has ripped through the modern business world at breathtaking pace, transforming it completely during my working life. I remember just a few years ago borrowing a screwdriver from reception at a hotel in Ecuador to unscrew the bedhead from the wall to get at the telephone jack so I could plug in and connect my computer to send an email to New York. I thought I was Alexander Graham Bell, Guglielmo Marconi and Tim Berners Lee rolled into one. And now massive leaps in connectivity speeds and bandwidth are opening up opportunities for the so-called *internet of things* that will transform our daily lives in ways that people with ossified analogue brains like me find hard to fully comprehend.

These new technologies hold enormous promise for good. But our dependence on the intricate apparatus of the internet has also ratcheted up our sense of knife-edge vulnerability. Hacking and cybercrime have become commonplace. We fret that terrible harm may be wrought on us by terrorists with malicious intent who are able to close down hospitals, poison our water, blow up our power stations, meddle in our elections and even nobble our pacemakers. Hacking is the cheapest form of warfare since the bow and arrow. You just need a socially dysfunctional teenager with a laptop.

Risk has digitalised. Nowadays, technologists abound as the industry has responded to this whole new dimension of security for executives and the enterprises they lead. Legions of data scientists are on hand to unravel, marshal, dissect and interrogate the vast oceans of data that have become the amniotic fluid – and the rap sheet – of all organisations. It has been a revolutionary transformation, not just in how corporations function but in what makes them fearful. The pace with which data sets and information systems became the critical spinal cord of organisations accelerated way ahead of our ability to protect them. This left an open door for thieves, hackers, cyber spies and extortionists to run amok. Ever since, we have been playing catch-up, trying to shut the door we left open, bolt it, install an alarm and make these most critical of assets safe from ever more sophisticated adversaries.

The most successful hackers rely not just on technical expertise but more often on a deep understanding of just how stupid otherwise intelligent people can be once sat in front of a computer keyboard or when idly playing with their phone. Businesses spend millions on intricate state-of-the-art Israeli anti-spy software, only for someone, who in every other aspect of their life would be cautious and alert, to click on a very obvious phishing email from what turns out to be a Moldovan cyber gang. In my early days as a newly minted CEO, we had an alarmingly close shave when a junior employee left, figuratively at least, the back door open while checking his email in an internet café in Albania. In the end, an embarrassing crisis was averted, and nothing was compromised. But it was a heart-stopping few days while we laboriously checked all our computer systems and dusted off our crisis management plans while restraining irate colleagues from beating their hapless – soon-to-be former – colleague to death in the stairwell.

The generation of executives running big companies today often struggles to comprehend the mind-warping complexities of the cyber world. For most of the problems that I spent my career grappling with, age and guile were usually an advantage. Some grey hair and grit under your fingernails was normally a help in understanding how to stay focused, not panic and discern a way out of the chaos. Now, it is often a disadvantage. The advent of cyber crime and the dread-inducing fear of your business being hacked means that otherwise seasoned executives can feel at sea amid technical complexity and the new lexicon of the digital world. Incomprehension is often compounded when an introverted IT expert is dragged blinking into the bright daylight of an emergency board meeting convened to figure out what to do before the share price crashes. Time to call in the new breed of supercharged millennials who actually understand this stuff and can explain it in terms their parents can too.

Cyber experts tend to be alarmingly young, somewhat obsessive and have the most eccentric of dress sense. They are not afraid of sporting the full suite of man-made fibres, often in lurid, clashing colours and styles. But they have to be tough. Even the most well-protected of companies and government departments get hacked with alarming regularity. They are often extorted by criminals who can effectively take them out of business by paralysing their IT networks until a ransom is paid in some form of hard-to-trace cryptocurrency. Dealing with the emotional fallout from panic-stricken analogue executives is not for the faint-hearted. Counselling them to resist the demands of scary extortionists while racing against the clock to get the business back up and running requires deep reserves of fortitude.

It seems an impossibly difficult time to be running a big company. As if figuring out which way the world is likely to pivot was not hard enough, there are so many other imponderables and risks pressing down on the headspace of the harassed corporate leader. Many CEOs are alpha personality types perfect for the bullish good times. They have over-developed reserves of self-belief, confidence and drive, and are able to keep many balls in the air simultaneously through sheer force of personality. Others take a more cerebral approach, lacking some of the public charisma perhaps but better able to make nuanced difficult decisions when the market – or fate – turns against them. Few are both. But most think they are, encouraged in their conceit by the propaganda machines that surround top-flight CEOs. And there are a few who should never have been there in the first place. At times of stress, they have to be steered out of the way – given a colouring book and some crayons.

Some major league CEOs find it hard to stay grounded when they spend their time shuttling from private jet to investor conference to board meeting to analyst call, surrounded at all times by sycophantic lackeys often too scared ever to tell truth to power. Many CEOs are pretending to oversee corporations that have become just too big to be managed through traditional pyramidal corporate hierarchies. They have almost certainly lost touch with the ground-truth of what is being done in their name. I once knew the boss of a major energy company who insisted on ice-cold air conditioning wherever he went. On a rare visit to equatorial Africa, the rest of his hotel had its air conditioning turned off so that his room temperature could be set precisely to his desired frostiness, otherwise he would have gone berserk. He did anyway. You know that someone that preoccupied by his own diva-like conceit is not asking the right questions about how the business is run.

The idea of an ever-more interconnected globalised world has been called to account in the past few years by the rise of populism, the re-emergence of superpower rivalry and the weaponisation of trade. This has resulted in mass cognitive dissonance for senior executives the world over who were reared on the notion of an ever more integrating world of borderless commerce. In reality, the nation state never went away. The three major crises of my professional life – 9/11, the global financial crisis and the COVID-19 pandemic – each revealed the primary role of national governments to protect the wellbeing of their citizens. And the most extraordinary economic phenomenon of our age – the complete transformation of China – has reinforced this sense that the world is far less cohesive than people like me occasionally imagined while we were looking out of the aeroplane window on yet another globe-circling business trip. In 1993, China had a significantly smaller economy than Spain. Since then, it has gone from being an exotic emerging market to becoming a competitor, then an adversary and, latterly, for some, the enemy. It is now on its way to becoming the largest economy in the world. Corporate strategists are having to rewrite acres of carefully constructed plans as the capricious reality of global affairs upends their forecasts and expectations.

Three mega-trends defined my time in the risk business. First was the runaway enthusiasm for globalisation that saw the phenomenal rise of Asia but was fuelled and enabled by a financial system that was as vulnerable as it was intricate. Second, the immediate impact and unforeseen consequences of the 9/11 wars in the Middle East, and the global fear of violent extremism of all kinds. And third, the digital revolution which has fundamentally reoriented how we define security. The risk business has ridden each of these waves with gusto and, in the main, risen to the challenge. These have been decades during which boundaries and barriers have been rolled back for international companies to reveal verdant new pastures – but ones with hidden perils. They have been years of growth and opportunity – but ones punctuated by remarkable reversals of fortune. A world of genuine and changing risks, turbo-charged by a total transformation in our use of technology. It has been configured by our declining ability to distinguish authentic danger from chronic over-reaction. For those of us who stumbled into the risk business at the beginning of this period, it proved to be fortuitous timing.

This may sound smug. It sounds like we prospered opportunistically and parasitically from others' misfortune or miscomprehension. To an extent, it is a justifiable criticism. This business has no doubt been the beneficiary of a more risk-aware and risk-averse world. It has also prospered from the exaggerated sense of peril and a reasonable expectation of litigation that causes many big companies to be gripped by an obsessive-compulsive disorder that requires them to document and mitigate every possible thing that might go wrong.

It is also why you should not really be in the risk business if you cannot maintain a healthy dose of humility and a sense of proportion and perspective. You have a fine line to walk. You have an obligation not to stoke the fires of people's anxiety by exaggerating danger and insecurity. But you have a perfectly legitimate right to highlight genuine peril and advertise sensible precautions. Airline safety briefings and condom manufacturers do the same. In most cases, potential customers can sniff out alarmists. They know crude over-dramatisation when they see it and will take their business elsewhere. It pays not to get too big for your boots.

In essence, you have the same relationship with the bad things that affect companies and those who run them as oncologists have with cancer. You would not wish it on anybody yet helping people when their world is collapsing is what you do, and you need to be good at it. For sure, there are moments when the drama and the thrill can obscure your judgement and purpose. But these are also complex businesses to run. They can test you to your limit and it is best not to believe too much of your own hype.

By now, the risk business has become a multi-billion-dollar industry. Most of the original independent players are still flourishing but they have been joined by a whole raft of newcomers. Many of these are still small start-ups, often former soldiers, diplomats, lawyers, spies and journalists, some with a touch of celebrity or notoriety, reprising their former skills in the commercial world. Most burn brightly for a while and then fizzle out when the guiding light of the founder's charisma and connections dims, or when the founder tires of the hard slog of running a business. Others acquire muscle-mass and are able to gain enough traction to move to a second generation and have a better chance of longevity.

The business is now dominated by much bigger outfits: giant insurance companies offering risk-related advice in addition to the assurance of financial compensation for when things might go wrong; management consultancies keen to add yet more strings to their bow now that risk management is regarded as a core competency of the successful, well-run corporation and not an auxiliary adjunct buried somewhere in the basement. Cybersecurity companies have proliferated as the threat has become manifest. Many have been launched into orbit by the frenzy of private-equity firms frantic to get a piece of the action. Accounting firms too are constantly trying to respray themselves as anything but auditors, adding the prefix *forensic* to all sorts of things in the hope they will seem a little cooler, a bit more chiselled and windswept. And at the more muscular end of the spectrum enormous security outsourcers provide the logistical support and manpower needed by governments and big companies, plugging the gap left by shrinking militaries all over the world.

As I withdrew from the business, the COVID-19 crisis was just starting – a kind of bookend to my career. On one level it is another form of crisis, albeit a big one, for which many of the core principles of how to cope are perfectly applicable. On another, the virus poses much bigger questions. It has caused the future to accelerate towards us, tossing into the air any certainties we may have had about how we work, socialise, shop, travel and how we want to be governed. The risk business will adapt to whatever altered reality emerges as vaccines allow us to regain some perspective on what has happened.

For nearly thirty years, I saw an industry grow and mature but hopefully retain some of that original Elizabethan buccaneering spirit that sparked it into life in the first place. It was a ticket to see places and meet people that I would never otherwise have encountered, and to run a business that was complicated, demanding and, when the chips were down, made a difference. It was also really great fun.

2

Lost in frustration

'OH MY GOD, THAT IS DISGUSTING. What the hell is wrong with you?'

That was my first and only encounter with the CEO of the financial services giant where I had recently started work, fresh from university. A knighted City grandee, he had spotted me as an obvious new boy and was about to greet me with the same patrician benevolence he might have shown to a new junior under-gardener at his country residence somewhere deep in the leafy home counties of southern England. But he had been stopped in his tracks.

Let me explain. After only a few weeks in the job, I had realised that this was not the place for me. I suspect my new employers were rapidly coming to the same conclusion, which probably explained why, after the initial induction period, I had been assigned to special duties at head office. Initially, I was thrilled. Special duties sounded great. I arrogantly assumed that I had been selected as part of an elite vanguard of high-potential superstars. It soon became apparent that special duties were confined to photocopying (which I was very bad at) and occasionally being sent to deliver documents to other parts of the headquarters – at the time, one of the tallest buildings in still low-rise central London.

It was on one of these message-delivering missions that I had my fateful encounter with the top man. Having deployed my full arsenal of human capability to deliver an envelope to an office on one of the upper floors, I got into the elevator to go back down. The British taxpayer had spent thousands of pounds on my university education. I knew why the Russian revolution had started. I also knew that Hitler was a wrong 'un and that Henry VIII might have had syphilis. I was evidently equipped for a stellar business career. There had to be something better than being a rather bumptious errand boy in an ill-fitting suit and shoes that gave me blisters.

In the lift, I bumped into an old acquaintance from university, who seemed to be thriving where I was floundering, which depressed me even further. We were alone and we chatted briefly before he got out just one floor down. As he left the elevator, he stopped briefly and reversed his bottom back through the closing doors. Bending forwards, he emitted a noisy, watery, blubbering fart.

At this stage, I should immediately apologise to readers of refinement or delicate disposition. Indeed, you may want to skip ahead a few paragraphs. Ordinarily, I would not dream of including such scatological material. But I do so not for the cheap ribaldry to be derived from flatulence but because of the special scientific significance of what happened next. The doors closed and I found myself entombed inside a steel cube, on my own with a gaseous cataclysm of similar toxicity to a World War One mustard-gas attack. It was invisible. But

I could chew it.

It was like being trapped in a Wilfred Owen poem. I was choking, drowning, guttering. I felt as if at any moment I would find myself gargling on the blood spilling forth from my froth-corrupted lungs. I stood on tiptoe, stretching my neck upwards to fresher air like a Japanese crane engaged in its elaborate mating ritual. It was so virulent I half-expected a crack team of bacterial biologists to abseil their way down the lift shaft to analyse what extraordinary chemical chain-reaction had occurred in my friend's intestines to trigger such a noxious outburst.

The lift doors opened. But my relief was short-lived as, to my horror, in strode the head guy. He beamed grandly at me and started to extend his hand in welcome. And then it hit him. Naturally, he assumed I was the culprit. For a moment, I thought about trying to explain that I was not actually responsible for this public-health monstrosity. But I realised that in all likelihood this was a career-terminating moment, and it was probably better for many reasons to keep my mouth shut until he managed to get out of the lift at the next available opportunity.

I retreated back to the office where I was based. My neighbour – another soon-to-fail trainee – looked up and saw my ashen countenance. 'Are you OK?' he enquired solicitously. 'Not really,' I replied, and slumped despondently into my chair. I stared out of the window at the view of London in the grey flat light of a cloudy autumnal morning. The tide had turned, and the great brown mass of the Thames was rushing past as the full force of the river headed for the sea. I decided to follow suit. It was time to move to Japan.

A few months after that fateful encounter with the poisoned gas, I found myself, by careful endeavour and some fancy footwork, starting work in Tokyo. It was not much of a job to begin with, but it was a fresh start and Japan was an exciting and, at the time, unusual place to be. I was mostly engaged in trying to explain the rules and regulations of the Tokyo stock market to foreign investors who were, for the first time, being allowed to trade directly in Japanese securities. The rules were exceedingly vague, opaque and contradictory. This meant it was impossible to be right but also – crucially – impossible to be wrong. This would prove to be a surprisingly valuable lesson for the future: as long as you are approximately in the middle you can get away with a lot. It all seemed to have worked out rather well until one day somebody asked me to take some documents to the CEO on the top floor. A déjà-vu-induced shudder ran down my spine. Surely some malign version of serendipity was not going to conspire for history to repeat itself. Reluctantly, I took the package, headed to the elevator and for the second time in my short working life found myself face to face with the big boss.

He too was born into the ruling class. But he was not the sort to head off late every afternoon in his chauffeured Jaguar to his gentlemen's club in St. James' to drink whisky while bemoaning the power of the British trade unions and the parlous state of the English cricket team. For him, high birth and privilege demanded a life of austere dedication. If he allowed himself any form of relaxation, it was to practise the ancient Japanese form of fencing known as kendo. On special occasions, he would go one further and compose a haiku, the non-rhyming, usually obtuse-of-meaning three-line poems beloved of Japanese aesthetes. He was a Samurai in a navy-blue suit.

I was to meet Kimura-san only a few more times in the years I was there. But each time I did, he made me feel awkward.

Not from what he said or did: he was always unfailingly polite in a clipped, unemotional sort of manner. But by the way he was. He was small of stature, but neat and compact. And despite his diminutive physique, his presence loomed large in the room. Being around him, I always felt too large, too sweaty, too cumbersome and physically unwieldy. It was as if I was just one clumsy stumble away from knocking over and smashing to smithereens the single piece of minimalist Japanese pottery that was the only decorative object in his office.

During World War Two, he had been a captain in the Japanese Imperial army. He was home on leave when the decision was taken for Japan to surrender following the bombing of Hiroshima and Nagasaki. The announcement was made by the Emperor Hirohito and formally broadcast to the nation by wireless. For those without access to a wireless, sets were installed in local town halls and other public places. Unfortunately, the emperor made his declaration using the formal court version of Japanese that was unintelligible to most of the population. To make matters worse, he couched the decision to surrender in terms so oblique that even those who could figure out the royal vernacular were perplexed. 'The war situation has developed not necessarily to Japan's advantage,' he announced, with remarkable understatement in a country that had just been nuked – twice.

Kimura-san heard the broadcast at a school hall in a suburb of bombed-out Tokyo. He understood what the emperor was saying, leapt on to the stage, drew his sword, smashed the radio set and told the assembled crowd that this was nothing more than American propaganda. He ordered them to go home and continue to endure and resist. Decades later, colleagues visiting from the United States would often detect behind

Kimura's impassive façade, a certain froideur.

Those early years in Tokyo were to be quite formative. One of the most enduring things I learned was about learning itself. Japan is notorious for its ability to befuddle visitors and foreign residents. But not me. With breathtaking over-confidence, I thought I had the place cracked. After only a few months in the capital, I was equipped with a ready answer for any of the common questions asked by foreigners contemplating Japan for the first time. What do the Japanese think about their royal family? How do they feel about being the only nation to have nuclear bombs dropped on them? How do they now regard the wartime conduct towards prisoners-of-war by the Japanese army? Why are their TV game shows so weird? I was smashing each question back over the net. If any visitor was rash enough to make any of these enquiries, I was quick off the draw with my own immediately available answer, confident that I had already diagnosed the inner workings of the national psyche. I was like a Japanese pot noodle. Just add water and I had an instant answer.

A year later and my comprehensive understanding had evaporated. I realised I knew nothing. My early fluency on all things Japanese had been replaced by a stumbling inarticulacy. Having jumped on the bandwagon of trying to elucidate everything anybody wanted to know about Japan, I now found myself backtracking badly. Where once I had been strident and confident, I now found my early assumptions crumbling under the weight of contradictory and confusing daily experience. I was now hedging my bets.

It was of course easy to mock any number of Japan's many idiosyncrasies. One of the easier targets came from Japanese designers' habit of adorning products with utterly random English phraseology incomprehensible to the purchaser. I once sat next to a very chic young woman on a train whose expensive handbag was emblazoned with the nutritional details of certain types of dog food and the beneficial impact they had on canine bowel movements. But the worst of its kind was an old lady working in a vegetable shop in a remote village deep in the Japanese countryside. She was undoubtedly very old. Japanese women are one of the longest-living population cohorts in the world. And like many women of her generation, she was almost permanently bent double at ninety degrees from the waist, only occasionally straightening up to her full, if diminished, height. When she did, she revealed the slogan on her T-shirt. SUCK MY COCK, it invited in bold capital letters.

Perhaps Japan is no more complicated and bizarre than any other country, but it is one of the most singular. Similarities with other nations are hard to find. Even when similarities do exist, as they do with their near-neighbours China and Korea, the Japanese are not keen to acknowledge them. Historical enmities run deep in North Asia. In any event, they enjoy and foster this sense of apartness, perpetuating the myth of uniqueness and encouraging the sense of a nation run on a different operating system from the rest of the world. The notion of a country apart is a key foundation stone of Japanese heritage myths. Japan's very unusual history of being deliberately cut off from the rest of the world for so many centuries explains some of why this carefully curated notion of a nation distinct from the rest persists. Equally, so does the national trauma of Japan's military rule in the twentieth century, its sense of being victimised by stronger powers, its military aggression in the Thirties and subsequent defeat in World War Two. But none of this entirely explains why Japan believes and acts as it does. This was a useful lesson as I embarked on a career in which there was to be a high expectation that I produce definitive predictions about world affairs, and pressure to deliver neat encapsulations illuminating the most obscure political complexities.

Occasionally, something will occur in Japan to upend the stereotype. I was once travelling home late in a Tokyo taxi, practising my embryonic Japanese language skills. The driver asked me if I was American. I explained that I was British. I was expecting the usual monologue on what an unusual place Japan was and how it must be baffling for me as a foreigner to adjust to life here. But the conversation surprised me. 'Of course,' he said. 'I thought so. We are just the same, you and me; the Japanese and the British.' I asked him why. 'Tea-drinking, island monarchies', he explained. Just when you think this is a determinedly inward-looking, self-absorbed country, it surprises you with such an intriguing assumption of cultural connectivity.

Long-term residents will advise you that you need to understand and speak the language to have any hope of understanding the Japanese mindset. That is easier said than done. Middle-aged Japanese male executives are notorious for never appearing to say what they really intend, hinting at meaning rather than spelling it out. When I was struggling to learn Japanese, I went to language lessons early every morning before arriving at work. I would burst into the office and launch forth in enthusiastic but appalling Japanese. My colleagues used to fall about laughing, not just at my incompetence but hooting with mirth as they explained that I sounded like their grandmother. How so, I would ask. Because you are speaking in whole sentences and using grammar, they pointed out – now reduced to uncontrollable comic hysteria by my ineptitude. I do not know why I bothered.

Japan struggles to reconcile its global heft with its own self-image as an introspective and self-obsessed nation. This was most palpable in the 1980s. Japan was the new super-economy, set to overtake the United States with its blend of state-directed industrial growth and single-minded drive for efficiency and market-share – all built on the endeavours of a hard-working and compliant workforce. Back then it seemed to have discovered a new genetically modified variant of capitalism. Many of the ingredients were the same but it was if they had been recombined in some new formulation, mixed by a team of white-coated alchemists in a secret laboratory buried deep in a tunnel system under Mt Fuji. Economists and management theorists beat a path to Japan, trying to discern what on earth was going on.

Japan then was in some ways like China now. Like contemporary China, its apparent success provoked both admiration and hostility. And as its success increased, the balance swung from the former to the latter. At the time, few people were predicting the remarkable transformation of China and all eyes were on Japan. Then, in the late 1980s, the bubble burst and the huge, speculative over-inflation of asset prices collapsed and drained the life out of the economy for a generation or more. Of course, in retrospect, a reclusive hermit who had spent the past fifty years secluded in a closed monastery on top of an inaccessible mountain in an unexplored corner of deepest Tibet should have known that the collapse was imminent. Well, I was there, and I failed to spot that, for all the over-exuberance and congratulation, the party was already over. I was not alone.

The decades since have seen Japan get by in a sort of perpetual twilight zone. It remains a huge economy with world-class companies. But it is weighed down by deflation, half-hearted attempts at reform and the shadow of unkind demographics as the population ages and the birth rate slips. It is also preoccupied by the seemingly inexorable rise of a brash, more assertive China just across the Sea of Japan.

You might assume that this switch in fortunes would have prompted Japan to turn inwards and become less inclined to deal with the rest of the world. They have form. Japan was in self-enforced isolation – *sakoku* – for over two hundred years. Foreign trade was severely limited, very few foreign nationals were allowed in and hardly any Japanese were permitted to leave. It was not until 1853 that the US government dispatched Commodore Perry with a naval squadron to force the opening of Japanese ports to US trade. You might have assumed that Japan would rediscover some of these isolationist impulses. It has not. Japanese companies remain some of the most globally ambitious in the world, albeit in a very specific and individual fashion.

For years now, Japanese companies, trading houses and the banks that bind them together have done business in almost every corner of the world. They are experienced and successful in a way that few other nations can ever hope to emulate. And yet they behave as if they have just arrived, fresh off the boat, blinking in the sunlight from some small town deep in the Japanese countryside, with no prior knowledge of what is going on in the world. This is, of course, complete nonsense. But it is a ritualistic way of behaving that has now become so ingrained that I think at times even the savviest of Japanese businesses believe it to be true. It is as if the self-perpetuated narrative of Japan as a small nation struggling to find its way in a strange and confusing world has been re-told so many times that even the most sophisticated operators adhere to it, despite all evidence to the contrary.

Sometimes the myth becomes reality. In 2004, I travelled for hours across the flat deserts of southern Iraq to visit an outpost of the Japanese self-defence force that had been established near the town of Samawah. Special parliamentary permission had been necessary to authorise Japanese troops to serve overseas in a hostile environment because Japan's post-war pacifist constitution had been designed to prevent Japanese forces slipping back into their nasty habits of the 1930s and '40s. To make sure their soldiers did not deviate from their pacific mission, they were to be accompanied at all times by members of Japan's diplomatic corps. Our role was to provide civilian protection for the diplomats even though they were surrounded by their own troops. In theory, by not being dependent on the Japanese soldiers for their security, the diplomatic team could be wholly independent in ensuring that everybody played by the rules.

In reality, everybody was living in very close quarters, in a small fortified camp, literally miles from anywhere in the middle of the Iraqi desert. And it would be hard to imagine a more wholesome group of troops. Their mandate extended to providing engineering advice on much-needed reconstruction efforts – repairing roads and bridges and fixing damaged irrigation systems – in this poor, war-torn corner of post-invasion Iraq. They were earnest and dedicated to their mission to an extraordinary degree. They also got along very well with the civilian security team, most of whom were former New Zealand special forces troops who had served in Afghanistan. It seemed like a token effort but in the convoluted logic of Japanese diplomacy, it was an important milestone. Japan remains one of the biggest aid donors to Iraq.

We were met by the impeccably dressed and polite commanding officer, Colonel Bansho, who showed us into his tent. Outside the temperature was almost as hot as it is possible to be as few places on earth are as boiling as an Iraqi summer. Inside it was hotter still. We were refreshed with scalding-hot green tea and a meal of vacuum-packed raw octopus to be eaten with chopsticks. When the conversation turned to the fact that I had once lived in Tokyo, I was treated as if I must have had extraterrestrial superpowers to have achieved such a remarkable accomplishment. Before we left, they gave me a commemorative medal denoting their mission to Iraq to say thank you for travelling for hours across a hazardous desert to see them. For once, the epithet of uniqueness was justified. This was Japan at its oddest – and most charming. A few miles in each direction, was murder and mayhem on an epic scale. But here, in this arid, scorched corner of southwest Iraq, was an oasis of Zen-like calm.

Advising Japanese companies requires some unusual skills. First, you must be prepared to listen intently to the lecture on how naïve and inexperienced they are and how little they know of the outside world even though you both know that this is not the case. An inordinate amount of head-nodding will be required. Second, you need to get used to the fact that a lot of the message that they want to convey is implied – often non-verbally – rather than explained. There is nearly always a backstory to what has really happened that must never be part of the formal account of the meeting. You are somehow meant to divine what it is they really want. Failing that, the gist of what has gone on and is now needed will be explained later, sotto voce to your Japanese colleagues, in the corridor on the way to the lift, once the formal part of the meeting is over. There are more efficient ways of commissioning risk management assistance but Japanese corporations in the main like to stick to this formula.

Many Japanese companies have a highly developed sense of responsibility towards the welfare of their employees when they are serving outside Japan. Most are willing to take outside advice on how to avoid the obvious perils and mitigate the more troublesome consequences of doing business in the far-flung corners of the world. And a few also have an extraordinary ability to get themselves into all sorts of often self-inflicted pickles. This combination is quite useful if you are in the risk and crisis management game. There is usually a never-ending supply of Japanese clients with one kind of problem or another. But discovering what the problem actually is takes patience. It often feels like I imagine doctors must feel when taking the medical history of a recalcitrant patient who cannot understand why he may be feeling below par. Only after careful and persistent questioning does the patient reveal that he smokes and drinks to excess and has not seen a vegetable for years.

Many organisations all around the world are similarly slow to admit at least partial culpability. I once had a client whose entire business in China had been replicated and effectively stolen by their erstwhile Chinese partner. It took numerous, interminable meetings, during which they went around and around the houses, before they eventually coughed up the truth. Often this reluctance to come clean arises when someone may have been indulging in a little extra-curricular *personal* activity. It is not a golden rule, but often extreme evasion and major gaps in the narrative are an indication that illicit knobbage has been occurring.

Japanese companies are no exception to this rule. I love Japan. I adore the exquisite nature of Japanese art, the serenity of a Japanese garden, the style and élan of metropolitan life in Japan's cities. I have sat on the upper slopes of Mt Fuji, looking from above onto the spectacle of a lightning storm playing out on the slopes below, the electric charge in the air creating an almost out-of-body experience. I felt like I had been touched by the sacred, at one with Japan's Shinto gods. But alongside the delicacy, there is delinquency. It is as if, having evolved to such a high level of aesthetic sensibility, there is an equal and opposite impulse to plumb the depths of depravity. A walk of spiritual purity in the stunning mountains of the Japan Alps or an afternoon watching the exquisite elegance of the tea ceremony is matched by wading neck-deep in the swamps of moral turpitude in the back streets of Tokyo's infamous entertainment district, Kabukicho.

Occasionally, the macabre underbelly of society presents a more sinister face. I was travelling in the Tokyo underground system at the time of the sarin gas attack one Monday morning rush hour in 1995. I escaped unharmed, but thirteen people died. The attack was carried out by Aum Shinrikyo, a strange doomsday cult. As in most countries when these kind of outlier incidents occur, the immediate response is to blame outsiders, to see it as some kind of external attack on the community and nation. When the perpetrators turn out to be home-grown, and willing to unleash such appalling violence on their fellow countrymen, it is much more unsettling, prompting soul-searching and self-reproach. But Tokyo, like most big cities, is incredibly resilient and, after a period of heightened anxiety and alert, levels of public concern would abate.

It is hard to know where Japan goes from here. On the one hand, it seems to have lost its capacity for reinvention that served it so well in the recovery decades after World War Two. It may have slipped into too easy a mediocrity. Corporate Japan is depressingly slow to embrace the right of women to enjoy equality of opportunity, free from traditional gender stereotyping. Of course, it is not for me – or anyone else – to lecture Japan on its cultural norms, but this seems to be one area where the notion of universal fairness and economic logic should coincide as the working-age population shrinks alarmingly. Yet the culture seems to be hamstrung by inertia and a reluctance to think that the immediate future may need to be different to the recent past.

In other ways, Japan's persistent attachment to centuries-old habits is its great strength. I flew to Japan in the immediate aftermath of the Fukushima tsunami and nuclear disaster in 2011. Tokyo, 150 miles from Fukushima, was still feeling the effects of numerous aftershocks. We had clients whose business continuity plans were suddenly being tested like never before. In the days after the earthquake struck and the tsunami hit the coast to such devastating effect, hundreds of expatriate staff were evacuated through fear of further dangerous seismic activity. In nearly all cases, this was excessive and unnecessary. But this happens a lot in the wake of a sudden emergency. Their Japanese colleagues were obviously not evacuated and for many it seemed like an odd response. In corporations that espoused the principle of equality among employees, it suddenly seemed as if priority protection was being given on the basis of ethnicity.

Talking to the Japanese authorities on the ground, I heard accounts of elderly Japanese citizens volunteering to go directly inside the damaged reactor unit where radiation levels could prove deadly for humans. They were willing to assist with the clean-up operation and make the reactor safe, in the knowledge that it would almost undoubtedly prove fatal. Their logic was that, as they were coming towards the end of their life, they were willing to take such risks for the greater good of the community. In short, they saw themselves as expendable. The authorities sensibly did not take them up on their offer. But I know of no other country where such an offer would be made on this scale in all sincerity. People may argue that this is an example of the same single-mindedness that has been deployed for far less honourable causes in Japan's recent history. But there is a rare nobility in this ancient notion of an older generation sacrificing themselves for the young.

The Fukushima disaster also highlights another aspect of how we find it so hard to process risk. In the aftermath of the disaster, the German government abandoned its nuclear energy programme, citing what had happened at Fukushima as one of the reasons for such a radical shift in energy policy. In reality, the Christian Democrats' need for the support of the German Green party may have been the more immediate reason, but there is no doubt that what had happened in northern Japan played a part. In reality, nobody died at Fukushima as an immediate consequence of radiation poisoning and the long-term effects in terms of increased frequency of cancer in the area are still disputed.

Looking back, I feel privileged to have started my career proper in Japan, after such a false start in London. Working in Tokyo in the 1980s was certainly an unorthodox business education. Cynically perhaps, it taught me how not to do things rather than acting as a shining example of best practice. It definitely taught me to pause and not rush to hasty, ill thought-out conclusions. It made me realise that there is a lot of space between the right and the wrong answer. All my subsequent experience of Japan has reinforced that same lesson in understanding that not everything is how it initially seems – not to judge a book by its cover. It was a revelation to realise that many people want to stay exactly the

3

By the rivers of Babylon

ONLY A PANE OF GLASS separated us. Not any old pane of glass, mind. But top of the range, bullet-stopping, thousands-of-dollars-a-sheet, hard-as-nails glass. If Mike Tyson was made of glass, this is what he would look like.

I looked again at the face on the other side of the car window. Was this what the world heavyweight champion of processed silica was protecting me from? He was about eight years old, dressed in a filthy soccer shirt and a pair of enormous, ill-fitting jeans. The T-shirt bore an urgent imperative to fly with a Middle East airline and was also emblazoned with the word Bale.

Bale, Gareth Bale. The Welsh wizard of footballing genius whose sporting pyrotechnics had earned him the cultish, obsessive devotion of millions of Real Madrid fans the world over. By contrast, this young lad roaming feral among the cars on Baghdad's busiest street looked like he had never been the object of anybody's devotion. And the vacant look in his eyes and the way his bottom lip hung away from his face suggested that he was not, as they say, playing with a full deck. Some countries nurture and care for their mentally ill. Some hide them away far from public view through shame or dogma. Others let them play in the traffic.

My attire fascinated him just as much as his fascinated me. A navy-blue wool suit, once-ironed white shirt and spotted silk tie – the standard uniform of the middle-aged corporate executive. But my bland, business uniformity was only the base layer, the undergarment for what I suspect had attracted his attention: my khaki Kevlar bullet-proof vest and a steel helmet so heavy that I had to make a conscious, muscle-tensing effort to stop my chin slumping forward onto my chest.

An interesting choice of attire for the Iraqi summertime. Outside, the temperature was heading towards 50°C. But inside the car it was almost arctic. The torpid, overheated air of the Middle East in July converted by an air-conditioning system of such carbon-consuming, climate-warping ferocity that even the most hardened of polar explorers would be left gasping for breath.

Our staring match continued. I smiled at him. For a moment, he did not seem to register the change. And then slowly, his downcast, slack mouth opened up into the most gorgeous, gleeful, life-affirming of smiles. For a fleeting moment, we shared that most primeval of human connections, the simple pleasure of happy mutual acknowledgement for no other purpose than that we both find ourselves here together in the oddest of circumstances at the same time.

And then there was a break in the traffic and our driver accelerated forwards, eager for the opportunity to get moving. I craned my head at an angle to try to prolong the moment. But he was gone. And as I watched him weave his way through the honking maelstrom of vehicles, his oversized trousers slipped down, revealing a view of his bum-crack grinning back across the street at me.

Our destination that morning was a government department and an appointment with the minister. Calling on politicians requires many things: enormous reserves of patience, a willingness to be kept waiting interminably and at times a self-shaming, skin-crawling capacity for sycophancy. Having spent hours and hours of my life all around the world (hours that I will never get back) waiting to see some very dodgy politicians, I have broken their dodginess down into a series of stereotypes.

First are the greedy. The gluttonous, malignantly avaricious, odious, sweaty accumulators of other peoples' money, whose sole justification for attaining public office is to rob, steal, burgle, purloin, embezzle, extort and misappropriate the usually slender resources of the state for their own ends. Second are the sadistic. The cold-eyed, frozen-hearted malevolent bad men (they are always male, before you ask) whose motivation is the opportunity to unsettle, intimidate and terrify. They usually say little but hint at fathomless depths of malice and cruelty.

Third is the incompetents. These folks are full of bluster and bonhomie, talking expansively and enthusiastically about their ambitious plans and achievements. The key giveaway is their repeated use of the word paradigm. Nothing gives away a total bluffer like paradigmitis. Occasionally, you catch their eye, and they realise that you have rumbled them, that you know they are, without a shadow of a doubt, utterly devoid of any modicum of capability to complete the simplest of tasks effectively. You both know that somehow some serendipitous alignment of luck and patronage enabled them to get the job. At this point, they have a nasty habit of turning into the second category and it is time to beat a hasty retreat.

I once met a government minister elsewhere in the Middle East who managed to fulfil each of these stereotypes simultaneously. Not only was he greedy, evil and incompetent, he also had a TV in his office tuned permanently and loudly to the children's cartoon channel. I have never felt so menaced while furtively watching SpongeBob SquarePants. And before you accuse me of falling for the stereotype, I have met politicians in mature, successful economies for whom being greedy and incompetent takes up so much of their mental capacity, they have no time to be evil. I am sure they would if they could.

Of course, there are many politicians who defy such characterisation. That morning in Baghdad, we were on our way to meet a government minister who did not fit the standard moulds. He was honest and realistic and seemingly motivated by a sincere, non-sectarian desire to improve the lot of his fellow Iraqis. But at the time the oil price was falling, and with it went Iraq's thin hope of an economic renaissance. And the seeds of the Islamic State insurgency had taken root a few miles away to the west. He did not last long. Within a few weeks of our visit he was gone, back to North London and an easier life among the Iraqi diaspora. At least he tried. Sadly, intelligence, duty and a latent sense of patriotism were not sufficient to navigate the brutal sectarianism of Iraqi politics.

The scale of the task was evident all around the city. Bombed out buildings still unrepaired from the 2003 invasion and overthrow of Saddam Hussein, intermittent electricity provision and atrocious public services. Next time you are stuck in traffic or a crowded train in London, New York or Tokyo, please try to remember that our daily lives are a rare form of paradise compared to what your average Iraqi experiences. Like almost everywhere, the ability of ordinary people to adapt is evident and astonishing. Markets flourish, kids go to school in smart crisp uniforms and normal life in abnormal circumstances finds its own odd rhythm in a city of nearly nine million people that has sat on the banks of the Tigris river for 1,300 years. Baghdad markets are quite an experience. I have never been anywhere where you can buy a live goat, a mobile phone, frilly underwear and a lawnmower (nobody has a lawn, by the way) all from the same stall.

But the appalling sense of thwarted potential was – and still is – palpable. Iraq is a country of vast hydrocarbon reserves. Most of its oil is easily accessible in vast reservoirs close to the surface. Much of it is known as *Basra Light* because of its low sulphur content, which makes it easy and cheap to refine into petrol. Iraq has plenty of oil, but its oil fields suffered from years of neglect under the Saddam era. What is more, oil fields need water to be pumped in to maintain the subterranean pressure that pushes the oil upwards. Southern Iraq, where the major oil fields are located, is parched.

The population, at close to 40 million, is not enormous and, you would hope, there should be easily enough wealth to go around. The population is also young – 60% under the age of 25. That is the sort of data that has economists drooling over their spreadsheets with the thought of all that latent productivity. The reality is not to be found in a spreadsheet. Millions of young people – particularly the fifty per cent-plus born male – under-educated and unemployed may look like an attractive statistic at some development bank headquarters. But when combined with corrupt and incompetent government and a ready supply of high-calibre firearms and top-grade narcotics it quickly becomes a toxic unstable brew.

Little has gone right for Iraq since Saddam was ousted. Sure, there have been moments when it seemed that the stars may at last be aligning, that a grudging truce between Iraq's sectarian factions was taking root and the country was finding some kind of political equilibrium, sufficient at least for modest progress to be made. Certainly, the worst of the violence has subsided, and oil revenues have flowed. But compared to the high hopes and public pronouncements that surrounded Iraq's liberation from the cruel tyranny of Saddam and his murderous family, modern-day Iraq is a place where it is easy to conclude that the capacity of nations to intervene in other countries' affairs and do good is vanishingly small, while their converse ability to do harm is infinite.

Commentators are always keen to pass judgement on major world events; to explain definitively why certain things happened and move current affairs quickly to the annals of history. Why we went to war in Iraq in 2003 defies such rapid categorisation. It remains unresolved, full of loose ends and messy contradictions. Afghanistan is much easier to figure out. Even if you vehemently disagree with the decision, it was a clear consequence of what happened in the US on September 11, 2001. Al Qaeda had attacked America. The Taliban government in Afghanistan provided a protected operating base for Al Qaeda.

Iraq is much tougher to puzzle out. Certainly, the ostensible reasons are inadequate at best and mendacious at worst. Saddam did not present the clear and present threat that we were encouraged to believe he did. Nor was it a devious plot cooked up by big oil companies to grab hold of the country's massive hydrocarbon reserves. But it might have been partly the consequence of a wildly ambitious neo-conservative notion that the US could re-order the Middle East, bring peace and democracy, prompt change in Iran, resolve the Palestine issue and create a new regional equilibrium in which America's long-term energy security would be settled for generations. Crazy, preposterous and hubristic as it now sounds, somewhere in that labyrinth of reasoning is the answer.

Normally, such ideas stay on the margins of government policy but in the febrile post-9/11 atmosphere and emboldened by the rapid battlefield defeat of the Taliban in Afghanistan, these ideas, disconnected from reality though they were, took hold in the minds of politicians, who felt all the normal rules had changed. Even with the benefit of hindsight, it is such a breathtakingly stupid plan, full of over-confidence and flawed logic. But I am constantly amazed at what ridiculous ideas are spawned by very smart people. This was not a plan put together by dunces, some of these people are whip smart. They just should not be allowed to put their ideas into practice, largely unchecked. And we should remember, for a while it seemed that the whole madcap idea might just work, when Baghdad fell easily.

I confess that I was one of the optimists. I first visited Iraq a few weeks after the end of the war. The problems were already mounting. The country was spiralling into sectarian violence and the newly arrived Iraqi returnees who had sat out the Saddam years in London, Stockholm, Amman, Tehran and many other capital cities quickly concluded that now was not the time for a triumphant return to their homeland. Many turned tail and hot-footed it back to safer refuges abroad. Middle-class professionals followed in their wake if they could, leaving the poor, the venal and the mischief-makers to wallow in the mire.

Western governments and agencies turned up in droves ready to build a new Iraq in their own image – only to retreat quickly behind concrete walls in well-guarded compounds as violence became endemic. The scene was thus set for a huge human petri-dish experiment, examining what happens to a repressed population when you decapitate the country and have little to put in its place, all recorded on camera for the world to see.

But fresh on the scene, I tried to find a compelling counter-narrative. I waxed lyrical about Iraq's tourist potential, given its Old Testament associations (nearly all of it happened here). I explained to anybody who would listen about the vast agricultural potential of a country irrigated by the mighty Tigris and the Euphrates – or at least what is left of them after their waters have been siphoned off in Turkey. And of course, all this development would be funded by selling the oil on which Iraq floats.

Of course, it now seems fantastical that a population made up of Arabs and Kurds, Sunnis and Shias deliberately pitted against each other for years by a ruthlessly manipulative and coercive state could easily and quickly adjust to plural democracy. It seems equally obvious that when that rapid transition from autocracy to liberalism did not work, then military occupation was not going to work either.

The optimists (I was no longer one) pointed out that the steadying hand of General MacArthur in post-war Japan and the allied management of West Berlin provided a blueprint for what might be possible. They are, I guess, valid examples. But they are outliers among the myriad instances of where Europe's retreat from empire has gone staggeringly wrong. Vain attempts to impose order militarily, to allow time for political process to mature, instead bred seething resentment and drove reasonable people to unreasonable violence. Violence begets violence. And once the spiral of recrimination takes hold, the adoption of ever more punitive measures by both sides proves hard to stop. A nasty, self-nourishing vortex of revenge ensues.

And that is the loop in which Iraq has spent much of the post-Saddam era. I have visited often, helping governments set up and secure embassies and deliver aid, helping construction companies rebuild war damage and later oil companies get Iraq's oil flowing again. Billions of dollars have been poured into Iraq's reconstruction and much of it has disappeared with little or no tangible benefit. I remember one project to build a new prison on the outskirts of Baghdad close to the Shia stronghold in Sadr City. In principle, this was a good idea. Iraq's Saddam-era jails were appalling. They were inhumane, breeding grounds for extremism, and in need of replacement. But construction of this prison soon stopped when the local militias in Sadr City realised that once it was constructed, they were likely to be among the first batch of inmates. They quickly prevented the construction crews from gaining access to the site and the project was abandoned. The city and the country are awash with such failures. The money that is approved by Congress gets dispersed and then, for whatever reason, the projects themselves never get completed. The place is littered with projects to build schools, hospitals and power infrastructure, paid for and then abandoned on the drawing board, the money melting away to reappear in somebody's bank account in Dubai or elsewhere. The US taxpayer, as well as the army and Marine Corps, have paid a heavy price in Iraq.

As a foreigner involved in the security business in Iraq, you are often portrayed as having been part of the problem. In the immediate aftermath of the US-led invasion, hundreds of security consultants flooded into the country, responding to a sudden and urgent need for their skills. The US administration had disbanded the Iraqi army and police force in what is now regarded as a premature and destabilising move. As thousands of diplomats, aid workers and all manner of reconstruction experts descended on the country, they found there was nobody there to maintain law and order and ensure they were safe. In fact, many of the former soldiers and police took off their uniforms and joined the militias and criminal gangs that were now responsible for the breakdown in law and order. The international security industry plugged the gap.

Inevitably, some of them were wholly unsuitable and should not have been there. The high wages that were, for a while, available attracted a fair number of charlatans and chancers. Many were overly aggressive in the way they behaved, and a minority acted appallingly. But most did not. Most behaved well and tried to conduct themselves responsibly despite being in a very odd situation. They were often on the front line of armed security in a country they knew little about, unable to speak its language and possessing little insight into the complex religious and tribal turmoil that was erupting around them. I declare my bias. But I think the vast majority of them behaved extraordinarily well, saved lives and kept the lifeline of foreign aid flowing. When the time came in 2008 for Iraq to play the only economic card it has and lure the international oil industry back to the country, it was this much – and sometimes unfairly – maligned group of men and women who in large part enabled them to do so.

During this time, the country has lurched from one crisis to the next, exchanging the suffocating embrace of American administration for the less evident but deeply ingrained influence of Iran. Much work went into crafting a constitution that would see political participation shared and balanced between Arab Sunnis and Shias as well as the Kurds. But fairness and firmness do not always co-exist easily, and Iraq was ill-equipped to deal with a visceral outbreak of Sunni-Shia sectarianism which provided a receptive base for Al Qaeda, and in turn the febrile breeding ground for what would become Islamic State. As rap sheets go, that is not great.

Iraq's agony has been drawn out. Around Mosul, the scene of the last major resistance by Islamic State in 2017, rival tribes, different imperial powers and people of different, often shifting, religious affiliations have been fighting each other for centuries with hideous brutality. It almost feels that the land itself is scarred with some form of post-traumatic pathology. When you dig deeper into what the country has endured and understand how little there is by way of prospects for the millions of unemployed Iraqis, you get some perspective on why so many people are drawn to conflict. Millions of young Iraqis have known nothing other than post-invasion Iraq. So many have had whatever hopes and aspirations they may have had thwarted. They have become habituated to the retributive cycle of communal violence and have watched as billions of dollars were stolen by politicians purporting to represent their interests.

For a great number of young people their chances of getting married and living a fulfilled sexual life are closed off by the lack of jobs and the chance of independence. Having seen all this at close quarters, the thing that staggers me is not why so many are tempted by terrorism but why it is so few. The terrorist recruiting sergeants tour the urban slums of Iraq. They promise – for young men at least – that a few hours' drive away in Syria is a life of respect, excitement,

manhood, money and marriage. I suspect there is often little
need to mention the obligation of Jihad. It may well be a cruel,
mendacious promise but you can see why they go.

Iraqi history is not for the faint-hearted. There is a lot of it,
and it is complicated. Helpfully, there are places that you may
remember. If you ever had the pleasure of attending Sunday
school as a child, then this will be familiar territory. South
from Baghdad, just off the overland route down to Basra,
is Hillah – once Babylon – on the banks of the Euphrates.
Sadly, there are no longer any hanging gardens. We once took
a wrong turn driving through Hillah. It was market day, and
our car was soon surrounded by sheep and goats and unable
to go forwards or backwards. We were very conspicuous, and
we sat there, just waiting for the local Shia militia to turn up
and kidnap us. Weirdly, I could not get the Boney M song,
'By The Rivers Of Babylon' out of my head. Eventually,
the irate goatherds moved their flock, and we resumed our
journey. My companion that day was murdered by a roadside
bomb in Baghdad a few weeks later, as he was taking some oil
engineers to a meeting at the Ministry of Energy.

Further south is Ur, birthplace of Abraham and home to
the amazing ziggurat pyramids. In the north, is the citadel in
Erbil, possibly the oldest continuously inhabited city in the
world. Further west is Nineveh, once the largest city in the
world and the busy epicentre of much biblical action. And
– most incredibly – the small town of Qurna claims to be
the site of the garden of Eden. Admittedly, modern Iraq has
not been blessed with the conservation gene or any sense of
architectural harmony. All of these places – with the possible
exception of Erbil – will be a major aesthetic disappointment,
scruffy and uncomfortably hot for much of the year. In fact,
you may well stomp back on to the tour bus, instruct the driver

to crank up the air conditioning and ask for your money back. But other countries have done far more with a weaker hand and made a fist of a tourist industry. Iraq could be great.

Topographically, much of Iraq is desert or the nearest thing to desert. The south in particular is so flat that you feel you can see the curvature of the earth as you come into land at Basra airport, the vista punctuated only by the wasteful gas flares from the multitude of oil rigs piercing the thin sandy crust to suck greedily on the unctuous, glossy slime that is the reason why we are all there in the first place. The vast reservoirs of oil do not respect man-made geographical boundaries and their vast web of underground arteries spreads east under Iran, south to Kuwait and west to Saudi Arabia. Each country, whatever its above-ground enmities, suckles from the same subterranean oil-filled udder. But for the few hardy tourists who include Iraq on their bucket list, the big draw lies far to the north in the semi-autonomous region of Kurdistan.

Mt Halgurd is in the northwest corner of Iraq, high in the bleak but beautiful Zagros mountains that stretch in an arc from the Strait of Hormuz in Iran northwards through Iraq to the Turkish border. Buried under deep snow for much of the year, a summer ascent of Mt Halgurd – Iraq's highest peak – is a joy. It is not a technically difficult climb, but it is made somewhat demanding by the rapid rise from near sea-level into the thinner air at 3,620 metres, and the lack of distinct paths.

The day I climbed the mountain, we took as a guide a local member of the Peshmerga, the Kurdish militia. He was the epitome of taciturn. A veteran of the guerrilla war waged in these mountains against Saddam, he strode vigorously to the top with no laces in his brown brogue shoes while smoking constantly. When I wheezed to the top sometime after him with a throbbing headache, he was sitting astride the summit cairn, puffing on yet another cigarette and fiddling with his revolver. I thought he might be about to execute me for general feebleness. Instead, he pointed out, across a deep valley to the north, a series of border posts dotted along the ridge opposite, denoting the Iranian border. It was alarmingly and uncomfortably close, given the stern way Iranian border guards tend to treat tourists who inadvertently cross over into their territory. The summit is littered with thousands of rusty shell casings, a reminder that this border, despite its inaccessibility, was the scene of fierce and almost entirely futile artillery exchanges during the Iran-Iraq war.

Getting to this remote corner of the country takes several hours of twisty driving, made slightly easier by one Archibald Hamilton. Hamilton was a New Zealander of Scottish descent who spent four years from 1928 to 1932 building a road through the mountains connecting Erbil to the Iranian border to open up a route through to Tehran. Have you noticed that wherever you go in the world, a Scotsman has been there long before you? A Scotsman and an Irishman, to be fair. The Scot will have done something practical like build a road, construct a bridge or impose martial law. The Irishman will have more likely tried to help start a revolution, written some poetry or, failing that, opened a bar. I sometimes fancy I can blame my half-Irish blood for my constant restlessness. It is the opposite to a fine wine. It does not mature by remaining immobile over many years. Rather, it fizzes discordantly in your veins, twitchy if kept still and agitating for you to keep moving for fear of the past catching up with you if you stay in one place for too long.

Life in these remote mountains, for centuries pinched tightly between the Ottoman and Persian empires, has always been brutal and hard. It has shaped the resilient, resistant nature of the Kurdish character. Their awful treatment at the hands of Saddam has only hardened their already profound sense of self-reliance. On the day I climbed the mountain, we had driven up from Baghdad and we stopped in a small mountain village to ask for directions. It was a run-down place; little more than a collection of crumbling houses crouched in the pass that connected one barren valley to the next. As we were looking at the map, an elderly lady rushed out of one of the houses. She started remonstrating with me and pointing repeatedly at the roof of her house. I had no idea what she was trying to tell me until a Kurdish companion stepped in and explained. It turned out that she thought our white SUV meant we were from some development agency. Her house had been bombed by Saddam nearly twenty years before. She was pleading with us to rebuild her home.

And that is where the truth lies – between the well-heeled traveller, filled with well-meaning curiosity but able to jet away after a few days, and an old woman who has been gassed, bombed and impoverished by the unconscionable actions of people far away for whom she is at best an unfortunate casualty of some grand geo-political game. I know, like and admire many of the people who tried to piece post-war Iraq back together. Not all, but many of them tried with honest and decent intent to make the best of a bad situation. But by then the die was cast. Too much harm had been done already by people either too remote from the consequences of their myopic decision-making or too hardened and cynical to care.

I am reminded of the words of Nick Carraway, F Scott Fitzgerald's narrator in *The Great Gatsby*, describing two of the wealthy protagonists in the novel: 'they are careless people, Tom and Daisy – they smashed up things and creatures and then retreated back into their money or their vast carelessness, or whatever it was that kept them together, and let other people clean up the mess they had made.'

The story of Iraq since 2003 is not about the struggle between good and evil; that is too glib and easy an answer. It is about the chaos caused by bad reasoning. Lust and greed have played a part, for sure. A big part. But they do not explain everything. It is also about the unintended consequences of mostly honourable people trying to make the least bad judgement in a series of no-win situations. No one realistically predicted that things would turn out as bad as they did. After the invasion in 2003, it is tempting to think that there may have been a chance to make some better decisions and avoid the subsequent descent. Again, in 2008, after the violence had subsided and the US administration handed over to the Iraqi government, it is possible that backing different political leaders might have been wise. But all of this comes with the wisdom of hindsight. Who reasonably foresaw that sectarian violence would rekindle Al Qaeda, which in turn would spawn Islamic State, and that Iraq would prove so fiendishly ungovernable? The conflict has now dragged on for so long, even after the US military formally left in 2011. It is impossible now to discern right from wrong, and hard – but not impossible – to believe that the same mistakes could be made again.

That is the reality of so many contemporary conflicts where moral absolutes are thin on the ground. For those of us who grew up in the long shadow of World War Two, this takes some getting used to. The war had ended seventeen years before I was born. My father, all my uncles, Mr. Bennet the newsagent, Mr. Hardwick the postman, Mr. Spittalhouse the butcher – indeed most of the adult men I knew in our corner of Yorkshire it seemed – had all been to war and returned victorious. They had fought a war where the distinction between right and wrong seemed clear-cut, and seventy-five years after it finished, it still does. That, I think, is the exception not the rule. I have never been to war. But I have picked my way through the debris of several and been left with many doubts and little certainty.

I am not impartial about Iraq. I have been a passenger on this journey, I have been fascinated by and indeed prospered from the turmoil. I hope, though, that I have been an honest and fair observer of what I have seen. But I am left uneasy. Uneasy because, for me, I can enjoy the adventure then climb aboard the next plane out, turn the page and move on. An old woman, her need for some small recompense for past, dreadful wrongs still unmet, and a confused young boy with his jumbled synapses weaving in and out of the traffic, are left to bear the consequences. There is some of Tom and Daisy in all of us.

4

In the shadow of our former selves

I FOUND MYSELF ONE HOT afternoon clambering over rocks on a granite escarpment high above the flat plains of northern Kenya. They were pre-Cambrian granite, half a billion years old. We were heading to a cave hidden among the rocks. A cave that until a few decades ago had been a bijou residence of the Mukogodo people, a group of hunter-gatherers who lived in these hills, subsisting on a diet of speared game and wild honey. My companions were their descendants, who earn their living now by different means, such as guiding people like me, inquisitive *mzungus* (white people), to visit parts of Kenya beyond the reach of the average visitor.

It had been an instructive day puzzling over one of the most vexed sources of friction and conflict in this part of Africa. To the uninitiated, this desolate and enormous land looked almost deserted as it stretched far away to a heat-warped, hazy horizon. But appearances are deceptive. What might appear to be an almost empty savanna is in fact contested land. Years of drought and over-grazing combined with an exploding population have made this apparent wilderness disputed territory. Different groups, from Maasai and Samburu pastoralists to Somali camel herders, each claim grazing rights to these lands. This brings them into conflict with each other, as well as with big landowners and with the conservation lobby who want to protect Kenya's indigenous wildlife and the tourism dollars that it attracts from the ravages of organised poaching. Add to the mix a few corrupt politicians keen to wrest some kind of venal advantage out of the situation and you have a highly combustible cocktail of competing interests.

This is not a theoretical conflict; it frequently erupts into bloodshed. On the walk up to the cave, we had stopped and chatted to a couple of young boys – teenagers herding vast numbers of goats illegally on conservancy land. They were friendly enough and dressed-up like dandies. In their traditional cloaks, multi-coloured bead-work jewellery and carefully braided hair, they were out to impress. This was certainly not for the benefit of the occasional random outsider like me. Rather, they were dressed to the nines in case a casual encounter at a watering-hole led to the possibility of romance. But the AK47s draped casually over their shoulders made clear that behind the handshakes, the smiles and the flirting lurked the possibility of lethal violence. As I had learned over the preceding days, any attempt at conflict resolution is intractably difficult. And there are all sorts of other reasons why this is no bucolic paradise. Female genital mutilation is still carried out among some of the communities that live here and efforts to eradicate the practice are sternly resisted.

But for now, I was less immediately concerned with heavily armed volatile adolescents or how to solve Kenya's resource wars and more preoccupied with keeping up with my guides. My attempt to follow them over the rocks was an acute reminder that decades of desk-bound inflexibility has withered the shock absorbers in my legs and calcified my spine, making every leap from rock to rock a painful, ligament- and vertebrae-wrenching jolt. But we made it and crawled into the mouth of the cave.

Actually, it was less of a cave and more of a horizontal slit. It was just big enough to accommodate a family group and protect them from the elements and the array of apex predators who might choose to go à la carte one evening and indulge in some human flesh – a little Mukogodo tartare – as a break from the monotony of impala and warthog. All day we had passed in close proximity to some big animals. Animals for whom we are a medium-sized meal. More than a snack but not the feast needed to feed an entire extended pride. This was a useful reminder of our vulnerability. Out here we are nowhere near the top of the food chain; just a middling mammal with below-average sensory capabilities and zero chance of outrunning hungry quadrupeds.

On the way, we had collected cannonball-sized spheres of desiccated elephant poo. Now we had settled into the cave, my companions set about lighting a fire using the bone-dry dung as tinder and two pieces of wood as a lighting mechanism. This was the moment I had been waiting for. Not far from here in East Africa is some of the oldest evidence of modern human existence, discovered in a cave much like this one. And here we were, recreating the exact same fire-creating skill that had enabled our anatomically recognisable ancestors to make that giant leap in evolutionary progress, flick the migratory switch and embark on the great expansionary journey out of East Africa that set homo sapiens on the road to global domination.

I was expecting an emotional thunderbolt. I waited for the psychic electrical charge that would roll back the centuries to forge this direct species-link to the earliest version of us. In the historical timeline of our planet, we are separated only by the merest flicker from our early ancestors lighting fires in African caves. Surely this was the moment to feel that great surge of ancient atavistic affinity.

Not a thing. The thunderbolt never arrived. My imaginative powers were numbed. Instead, I was crouched uncomfortably in a hot crack in the side of a hill. I was surrounded by piles of marmot shit, watching two guys fail to light a fire. They were going for it hammer-and-tongs, but to no avail. They were rubbing the long cylindrical stick fashioned from hard wood between the palms of their hands so that the pointed end bored into the softer flat piece of wood. Plumes of smoke billowed out chokingly into the confined space of the cave. But there was no spark to light the elephant poo that they had packed around the point where the two pieces of wood came into contact.

They swapped over when their hands got tired and started to blister, before impatiently swapping back, blaming each other for the ignition failure. I tried to be helpful by rearranging the poo, only to be told politely but firmly to get out of the way. Kenyan masculinity was at stake here and this was no time for a *mzungu* to get involved. After what seemed like eternity, the smoke eventually gave way to a spark. They blew gently and coaxed it into flames. The relief was palpable; warrior pride had been upheld, but only just.

And then the connection was made. Of course, it was not the process of staging a fire-lighting facsimile that was going to make the connection. Not at all. It was their embarrassment at not being able to do so that is identical. Exactly the same today as it was hundreds of thousands of years ago. Embarrassment: along with love and anger, one of the most enduring of human emotions. In that moment, in the shadow of our former selves, I felt the hot breath of ancient times on my neck. I sensed the long arm of history reach forward and fold me gently back into the deep past, to where it all started. Now I knew who these people were.

It is easy to romanticise Kenya. Tourists by the planeload descend on the place. Sold on the landscape, the animals and the whole safari-chic fantasy of frontier adventure, they arrive khaki-clad, with their necks drooping under the weight of dangling cameras and binoculars. Lensed-up like war correspondents, many come for the opportunity to encounter wild animals at close quarters. Others come looking for a little Happy Valley debauchery, trying to recreate the infamy of the aristocratic decadence enjoyed by mostly British colonial settlers in Kenya's magnificent Rift Valley in the first decades of the twentieth century. And others still are drawn to its beautiful Indian Ocean coastline with its magnificent beaches and relaxed vibe. Even those who come not to recreate the colonial Out of Africa fantasy but to do good as part of the swollen ranks of the NGO brigade, risk falling into the trap of pushing the white saviour's stereotype of what they want Kenya to be and not what it is. I am guilty on all counts.

The reality for most Kenyans is, of course, radically different. Most are bystanders and observers of other people's notional make-believe version of their country. They do so with enormous tolerance and unfailing politeness – what you might expect from a people renowned for their hospitality and formal good manners. What is distinctive about Kenya is that at least two radically different versions of the same country exist side-by-side – the outsiders' idealised version of wild, frontier Africa and the local Kenyan reality of an increasingly urban nation grappling to secure its place among the ranks of fast-growing industrialising economies.

Sometimes they intersect. In September 2013, the Westgate shopping mall in central Nairobi was attacked by gunmen from the Al-Shabaab terrorist organisation with links to Somalia. Sixty-eight people died in the attack. Al-Shabaab has long been in conflict with the Kenyan Defence Force, due in part to Kenya's significant role in the African Union military mission in Somalia. This was not the first time that Kenya's vulnerability to terrorism had been laid bare for the world to see. In 1998, Al Qaeda had attacked the US Embassy in Nairobi, with spectacular consequences. Nor would it be the last. Eighteen months later, Al-Shabaab attacked Garissa University College in northern Kenya, massacring 148 students.

But there is an often-cruel calculus to what makes an event globally newsworthy. The Westgate incident lasted long enough for international news crews to get there, and when they did, they had easy access to the site. That the Kenyan soldiers who were sent in to take back the building were alleged to have prolonged the attack in order to systematically loot the shops in the mall added spice to the story. Tales of venality and corruption act as an accelerant to any narrative and, in this case, they reinforced the prejudiced view of local Kenyan incompetence that plays to the inherent bias of foreign audiences.

A number of foreign civilians took matters into their own hands and, with extreme bravery, entered the building to evacuate shoppers trapped by the terrorists. This added an additional newsworthy sub-plot of civilian heroism. There were countless examples of local Kenyan bravery that day, but these stories are of no interest to the British tabloids. I was in a board meeting in London when a message was passed to me discreetly under the table explaining that two of my colleagues – a friendly Irishman and a taciturn Welshman – had slipped into the Westgate Centre after the attack had started. They had initially entered the building to rescue a client and his family from a restaurant on the top floor. Despite the presence of armed terrorists, they had found a way in, made their way up a service staircase and escorted the distressed family back out to safety. But they knew they had been forced to leave many others behind. These families were now trapped by the terrorists, who were working their way up through the centre, floor by floor, shooting and killing as they went. They made the decision to go back in. Over the next few hours, they evacuated scores of people under the noses of the terrorists, moving them as rapidly and quietly as possible down a stairwell at the back of the building. It was an act of extraordinary courage. For the rest of the board meeting, I was given regular, covert updates on their progress while struggling publicly to concentrate on the complexities of a discounted cash-flow calculation. Not for the first time, I felt stuck on the wrong side of the managerial divide.

Westgate was a direct attack on a soft target that crucially included among the casualties a number of non-Kenyans. That is the harsh, unpleasant reality. Africans killing Africans creates little more than a flicker of international media interest. Add in dead white people and you have a story. Years later, Westgate remains an iconic moment in the tragic canon of urban terrorism. The attack on Garissa University is almost entirely forgotten outside Kenya.

Whatever the rights and wrongs of its infamy, the Westgate siege intruded rudely into the popular public perception of Kenya as a nation of red-robed, spear-carrying people living in harmony with nature in a land of bountiful splendour. Instead, they saw a gritty city where the extremes of wealth and poverty coexist intimately, where the public defenders cannot be trusted, and armed terrorists brazenly attack innocent bystanders. For a while the tourist numbers declined, and the narrative changed. And when the outcome of the 2017 elections was contested, and resulted in a terrible outbreak of communal violence, then all the old prejudices about post-colonial Africa were trotted out.

We were fed the usual lines about a nation where tribal loyalties count for more than any sense of nationhood, where politicians are motivated only by the malignant chance to feather their own nest with little regard for the wellbeing of the people who vote for them, where the latent capacity for spontaneous violence lurks just below the thin veneer of social normality. It is not that any of these points are wrong absolutely – each is to some extent kind of true – but that they are massively insufficient to explain how a country like Kenya truly operates.

The high drama that draws the fickle attention of international television is not representative of everyday reality. These are outlier events, not normal life. There are other countervailing forces at work here that stop these otherwise destructive elements driving the country into anarchy. Kenya is resilient. Most Kenyans do not riot or steal. They do not sympathise with or support terrorists. They get on with their lives, work hard and care for their families. Over time this is why the country rights itself after these kinds of shocks. It has a quiet but powerful momentum for progress, stability and normality, along with a deep-seated ability to self-heal that sees the country bounce back time and again.

I have seen this at close quarters. In 2019, Al Shabaab returned to the streets of Nairobi, attacking an office and hotel complex in the city centre. This time it was very close to home. My colleagues were at work in the office block that was attacked. An Al Shabaab gunman entered the building, probably intending to position himself on the roof as a sniper as the rest of the gang attacked the hotel a few doors down. He shot dead two people in the adjacent office and then entered ours. By the time he did so, everybody had retreated to a room at the back of the office and was hiding under a table. They stayed still for what seemed like an age as he scouted the office looking for more victims. He came perilously close – they could hear his breathing – but he never spotted them and left.

By staying still and quiet they survived. For many of them, they had to resist their strong, almost-overwhelming, impulse to run, to try to flee down the fire escape. Had they done so, they would have been seen and pursued. But in those kinds of tense situations, the instinct to take flight is incredibly difficult to suppress. Even after the gunman had departed, they had to remain still for several hours as gunfire and explosions raged outside, and other people were shot dead as they tried to flee. They remained in hiding, uncertain if he or others would return. It was a traumatic ordeal, and their collective bravery and composure was extraordinary.

I arrived a few days later. I knew it had been a profoundly upsetting experience for all of them. At moments like this, your words of thanks and gratitude ring hollow. They sound inadequate and facile. It always feels as if you are intruding. And writing about it a long time after the event, it still feels intrusive. You can sympathise and try to find the right words. But you weren't there, you don't know what if feels like to have lived through the ordeal. However sincere you are, however much you want to help, you know that there is part of what you are doing that is resented by the people who have suffered together. And if you are truly honest, there is part of you that resents them for making you feel excluded. The emotional politics of grief and trauma are complicated.

Terrorism is uncommon in Nairobi even if it does attract a lot of attention when it occurs. Most of the city's five million people live lives largely unaffected by these kinds of incidents. Nairobi started life as a rail depot when the British built a railway connecting inland Uganda to the port of Mombasa on the Indian Ocean coast. The city became the centre of British rule during the colonial period. It remains not just the capital of Kenya but the regional hub for the wider East African region, home to multiple companies, NGOs and international institutions like the United Nations. The place always feels like it is undergoing a building boom, with many high-rise office blocks, funded often by Chinese investors, changing the landscape and the pace of a once more verdant, less vertical city.

Nairobi has all the contrasting hallmarks of a modern African city. A vibrant, well-educated middle class is looking to shake off some of Kenya's inherent conservatism to successfully craft a more dynamic, entrepreneurial future. But Nairobi is also home to some of Africa's biggest slums, housing over two million people. Kibera is the most well-known. It is a staple of nearly every conscience-crunching documentary on African poverty and often visited by international celebrities seeking to raise money for charity. Yet nearly all of Kenya's two million annual tourists give it a wide berth. Estimates vary widely on how many hundreds of thousands of people live in Kibera, most of them in over-crowded 12' by 12' shacks without sanitation or reliable electricity. A hard life is made worse by a lively drugs business and the consumption of the local home-brewed spirit, *changaa*. The government has tried to regulate *changaa* production and prohibit it being laced with ethanol for extra potency, a practice which probably gave rise to its nickname, *kill me quickly*.

At night, gangs of quite small children leave Kibera and the other Nairobi slums and roam the city. I once arrived late at Nairobi airport. The arrivals terminal had recently burnt down, and the immigration process was even more tortuous and time-consuming than usual. By the time I was heading into town, it was past midnight, and the streets were quiet. We turned a corner and immediately heard a squeal of brakes and the sound of a vehicle skidding. About 50 metres ahead, a car had hit a young boy. He was about eleven years old. By the time we arrived, he was already dead. I looked down at his face. He was beautiful. He seemed so peaceful, with no hint of the extreme violence that had been wrought on him minutes before, as he ran across a darkened street and his short life was extinguished prematurely.

Lots of people were already on the scene, tending to him and an ambulance had been called. People often seem to materialise from nowhere in the African night. We stopped and asked if we could help but my driver was very reluctant for me, a white person, to get involved. Once we knew there was nothing useful to do, we left. Later, I ended up tipping my driver a huge amount of money when he dropped me off at my hotel. It may have been some kind of proxy atonement or hopelessly inadequate penance for this vulnerable young lad being out on the streets at night. I had an angst-ridden night of agitated dreams about my own children.

Slum life is not all death and deprivation. Kibera and the like are also hotbeds of creativity, with their own music scenes, theatre groups and artists. Kids go to school neatly turned out in their uniforms and passionate, determined people improvise employment in all kinds of ways. This passion and creativity spreads beyond the fluid boundaries of Kibera. Indeed, the *matatus* – Nairobi's scantily regulated bus transportation system – display a combination of entrepreneurial invention and flamboyant artistic expression as they move around the city with music blaring from their garishly themed interiors, their drivers touting for passengers.

It is hard to describe Nairobi and Kenya without descending into one cliché after another. Beauty contrasts with horror, dynamism with despair. To cast Kenyans as victims is to succumb to yet another unhelpful form of post-colonial stereotyping. The story of this complex, contradictory nation is a series of alternative realities. They shift in and out of focus as different versions of Kenya reveal themselves.

The country is in a tough neighbourhood, not least for its northern border with Somalia. Somalia is home to Al Shabaab, and Kenya has been the target, not just of Al Shabaab attacks on the general public in Nairobi, but also by raiding parties marauding south down Kenya's coast, kidnapping and attacking civilian targets. Kenya's coast feels quite different from the interior. This is East Africa's Islamic fringe, with Arab, Persian, Omani and even Chinese influences over the centuries, which have combined to create a special and distinct atmosphere.

Kenya is not one of the world's kidnapping hotspots, but a small number of highly publicised kidnappings gave the coast, for a while at least, an unfair notoriety. Rational assessment of risk gave way to an exaggerated sense of fear. I spent time with a remarkable British woman who had been kidnapped while on holiday in Kenya and held hostage for months on end in Somalia. She had endured significant hardship and misery yet had coped and recovered remarkably well, at least superficially.

She had certainly discovered levels of toughness she perhaps did not know she had. She demonstrated a stubborn refusal to be cowed by her captors and had put up spirited defiance in the face of terrible provocation. When it mattered, she was tough beyond words. And the same applied when she was eventually released. I suspect that she had survived by forming a hardened core deep inside. I have seen this with other survivors. They cope by closing down some part of their emotional centre, by shuttering part of themselves so tightly that it remains inviolate. And when they are released, they find it hard to re-emerge from that armoured shell.

Kidnapping is one of the most traumatic of crimes, depriving somebody of their liberty in order to exert some kind of leverage on their loved ones. It is an ancient form of cruelty and the thought of it still strikes fear into the hearts of all but the most cavalier. For more than a quarter of a century, I have followed the course of hundreds of cases of hostage-taking by criminals and terrorists all around the world. I have learned the techniques and judgements deployed by close friends and colleagues as they advise on what is required to secure the safe release of victims. It is an art and a science, involving identifying the motivation and intent of the hostage takers and navigating a delicate, intricate course through to a safe release when there is so much at stake.

After decades of working alongside kidnap negotiators, the only thing I know with certainty is that I could not do it. I do not have the psychological fortitude to cope vicariously with other people's intense anxiety. It sounds glamorous and at times it is. The heartfelt gratitude you receive from a family when someone whom they have almost given up for lost is safely returned to them is addictive. But it is difficult, disruptive, stressful, emotionally draining and sometimes tedious work. And after all these years I remain in awe that some people can do this for a living over many years.

Kenya has also been battered by the side winds from another one of benighted Somalia's problems: piracy. For around ten years in the early part of this century Somali pirates attacked and disrupted shipping in the Gulf of Aden, seizing ships and ransoming their crews and cargoes. What started off as attempts by Somali fisherman to discourage large foreign trawlers from pillaging their fishing grounds turned into a multi-million-dollar criminal enterprise. The pirates were mostly young men, addicted to *khat*, a locally grown plant that produces a narcotic stimulant when chewed. They are dispatched by gang leaders on flimsy motorised skiffs, often with only enough fuel for an outward journey far out to sea. Without the option of a return to shore, they were highly motivated to seek ships that they could board and take over. As ship's defences became more effective, they started making increasingly audacious attacks on increasingly large vessels, including one over-ambitious attempt to wrest control of a French destroyer. Kenya became the jumping off point for much of the international naval response and suffered from the creeping influence of pirate activity. It was also the forward operating base to advise ship owners on how to handle the organised crime syndicates running the piracy through a network of connections in East Africa and the Middle East.

Helping combat piracy was a tough business but there were some lighter moments. For months on end, we worked in Nairobi through a Somali intermediary – a lawyer – to establish the wellbeing of the crew from an oil tanker hijacked up the coast from Kenya in the Gulf of Aden and taken captive in Somalia. It took ages. These interactions are always painstaking and delicate, as you try both to establish some kind of mutual confidence and to figure out whether the counter-party can actually deliver what they claim. This was no exception, and was further hampered by the language barrier. At the outset, the lawyer spoke almost no English and a translator was needed. This always frustrates the process. Luckily, the lawyer was a quick learner, learning the language on the job from the two negotiators charged with working to secure the crew's release. By chance, both Dave and Tony were from the same part of Yorkshire and spoke with the same distinctive north country accent. After nearly a year of laborious dialogue, the Somali lawyer's English had improved immeasurably. He would ring up and say: 'Heyup lads, what the fook's happenin?'

Kenya regularly appears on the numerous investor lists of countries that are about to take off – one of Africa's equivalents of Asia's tiger economies. This country is too big, too young and beset by persistent drought to survive on its tourism dollars alone. It should and can have a prosperous future, much of it no doubt financed and built by China. But there will continue to be many points of conflict where competing versions of Kenya collide. Even projects that elsewhere might be straightforward take on a vexed complexity in Kenya.

I have seen what happens when someone wants to build a power station on a pristine stretch of coastline, when someone else wants to build a wind farm that disrupts the flight patterns of rare vultures and when there is a proposal to build an oil pipeline to the coast that crosses land of disputed ownership. There is nothing unique to Kenya in these kinds of disputes; they happen the world over. But what is particular to this place is that they strike at the heart of Kenya's national schism: the romanticised wilderness that we want to preserve in aspic for future generations and, by contrast, the dynamic emerging industrial economy that will give 50 million Kenyans some of the opportunities they deserve. This being Kenya, the disputes are taken up right around the world by the self-appointed foreign guardians of the country's pristine integrity. Some workable synthesis of the two often seems frustratingly out of reach.

For too long, the debate about how to preserve Kenya's wildlife and tackle poaching was dominated by non-Kenyans. The interests of local communities were acknowledged but deemed secondary to the welfare and conservations of animals, or at least that is how it seemed to people who felt marginalised and disenfranchised in their own land. Belatedly, there is a recognition that sustainable, productive, profitable conservation requires a different approach. The two versions of Kenya – lions roaring at dawn on the Maasai Mara and Kibera children scavenging among open sewers – are not separate countries. There is an acknowledgement of sorts that their mutual prosperity is co-dependent. It is a hard road.

It is easy to put all of this out of your mind on the high ridge above the planes of Laikipia. The fire was eventually lit in the cave, honour restored, and tea brewed. Noisy, rumbustious Kenya seemed a lifetime away while sitting on a rock looking out over that extraordinary landscape in the late afternoon sunshine. My guides had that wonderful African quality of being entirely happy to sit for ages in silence. I resisted the temptation to talk and pester them with yet more questions. I gave myself over to the experience of watching the landscape shift tone as the light started to fade, feeling the last of the warm sun on my face and drinking my tea. Down below the escarpment, there was a great slab of flat granite about half the size of a football pitch. In my reverie, I conjured up the scene of large numbers of early homo sapiens mustering there, ready to depart on the great exodus trek that would see them emerge from Africa and populate the globe. There would be a stern sergeant-major type in charge with a clipboard.

'Right, you lot, listen up. I am going to tell you where you are going.

'First of all, the miserable bunch who took ages to light the fire. Yes, you lot, now standing there looking at your feet, you're off to England. You'll fit in well there – they are embarrassed about something or other all of the time'.

'And you, the gloomy bunch at the back, you're going to Scotland.'

'But sir, we don't want to go to Scotland. We heard the south of Spain was rather nice at this time of the year.'

'Shut up, you're going to Scotland. Anyway, after a while you can probably go on from there to America.'

'What's America?'

'I don't know. But apparently it's going to be fantastic'.

'What about us?'

'You have to stay here. In a few thousand years, this lot will be coming back on holiday and you can show them around the cave where your granny used to live.'

Despite my best efforts to understand all aspects of modern Kenya, I am pulled back – conscious of the outrageous hyperbole and exaggerated sentimentality – to this sense of Kenya as the cradle of our existence. I'll be back soon. People like me are drawn time and again to Kenya. It is a fascinating, changing, hard-to-grasp, split-personality of a country. Yet it goes deeper than that. It tugs at our heart strings in a way few other places do. Maybe it is because we are coming home.

5

Cocaine and Cornettos

'YOU WANT ME TO DO WHAT?' I spluttered.

'Go to Medellín and find out what's going on?' I repeated.

'Are we sure that is the best approach?' I equivocated.

I was sitting comfortably in my office in New York one morning when my boss from London called, instructing me to go to Colombia as soon as possible. He explained with customary bravado that it would be all quite straightforward and that I was just the right man for the job. Back then, in the mid-1990s, Colombia was not what is has now become. It was still a byword for kidnapping, extortion and assassination. Nowadays, much has changed for the better, and it has become the easy copy-filler for every travel supplement, website and luxury lifestyle magazine. In those days it was a long way from being the hot new destination du jour for the discerning eco-traveller.

I was not keen to go. I had my hard-won credentials as the most cowardly person in the company to preserve. I could not go into the lion's den, onto the front line. I was a back-room kind of guy, a strategist not a tactician and certainly not someone who went very close to the flames. But as my boss deployed an artful combination of flattery and coercion down the phone, I realised that I was running out of excuses. It was time to stand up and be counted.

I knew a little about Colombia. Its beleaguered government was locked in two wars that it was by any measure losing. The first with an assorted group of left-wing paramilitary groups – the FARC and ELN among the most conspicuous – who effectively controlled vast areas of rural Colombia where they, not the government, were in charge. And second, the war with the various cartels that manufactured and controlled Colombia's infamous main export: cocaine.

To complicate matters, the FARC and other groups had joined the cocaine supply chain. The combined resources of some of the oldest and best organised terrorist groups in the world with the money-spinning ruthlessness of the illicit narcotics trade made the task facing the government in Bogotá almost impossible. The fact that so many of Colombia's political class were in one way or another complicit in perpetuating the misery for their own ends meant that the chances of the country's long nightmare ending were not good.

Eventually US support, along with some stiffening of the Colombian backbone, would prove decisive in tackling both scourges. But at the time, the United States' main contribution was to provide an insatiable demand for Colombia's white powder. Back then, cocaine was less ubiquitous than it is now. It was still essentially a middle-class drug, almost a respectable recreational supplement to fine wines and cocktails. It was the pick-me-up of choice for investment bankers on Wall Street, actors in Hollywood and the occasional politician in

Washington, all safely insulated from the degradation, cruelty and extreme violence that was intrinsic to its journey from leaf to nostril.

So, just over 24 hours later I was sitting on a plane leaving New York's JFK airport for the flight south to Bogotá. I opened the newspaper, and, by coincidence, there was an article on Colombia's drug industry. It read like an eye-witness account from Dante's seventh circle of hell. What was I doing? I had not joined the risk industry to be put in harm's way.

I was certainly quite enjoying the dinner party kudos of working with people who did extraordinary and brave things – helping negotiate the release of hostages in far away and dangerous places, for instance. But I was keen to do so without actually having to do any of it myself. I was very happy vicariously trading on other people's heroism, wallowing in the warm, reflected glory from colleagues whose credentials as men and women of action I hoped lent me a kind of faux glamour by association. And to be honest, I had become alarmingly adept at deftly appearing as if it was sort of me that did this stuff without ever explicitly saying so. It was a skill that – in the cold light of day – I was not particularly proud of. But I was good at it.

As the plane bumped over the Andes before beginning its descent into Bogotá's El Dorado airport, I braced myself for what was about to happen. I imagined being whisked at high speed through burnt-out neighbourhoods, dodging the hit squads of evil ninjas that would have been sent to intercept me before arriving at my heavily fortified hotel. I looked out of the window. A long, thin, low-rise city, nestled along the side of a forested Andean ridge, hove into view. The plane landed with a thud in the thin mountain air. I was as ready as I was ever going to be.

A few hours later and my cheery taxi driver dropped me off outside a delightful restaurant situated in a pretty square a short journey from my hotel. A hotel, incidentally, that was playing Brahms in the lobby when I had checked in an hour before. Friends and colleagues called to me from the restaurant terrace, greeting me warmly as they called the waiter over to order another bottle of Argentinian red.

This was not what I was expecting. Having anticipated the worst, the reality was completely disarming. It was a delightful evening. A beautiful location, great food, and I made many new Colombian friends over conversation that ranged further and wider than its New York or London equivalent. It was an effective primer in the multiple contradictions that make up Colombia. At the time, I thought these people must be in denial about what is happening in their country. Later, I was to learn that it was the very proximity to danger that gave Colombians their determination to live life to the full. But that kind of insight was way in the future. For now, I was just enjoying myself.

A few hours later and I was escorted back to my hotel, garrulous – if not mildly hysterical – due to the combination of nervous tension released, a long journey and the copious quantities of Malbec that I had consumed with evident enthusiasm during the course of a long evening. The next morning, I woke groggily and remembered why I had come here in the first place: a client with a complex and acute problem that, somehow, I was meant to help them fix. But before I turned my attention to what I was paid to do, I was to experience a side of Bogotá life completely at odds with the charming metropolitan chic of the previous day's dinner.

That evening I set out with a friend to visit a hostel and rehabilitation centre that we were helping fund for Bogotá's many street children. The hostel was located a stone's throw from the previous evening's restaurant. But it was a universe apart. Located in a tough neighbourhood on the border between the more affluent, and safer, northern districts of Bogotá and the southern, poorer end of the city. A part of the city that most expatriates and wealthier Colombians avoid at all costs, particularly after nightfall. To give me a sense of the scale of the problem that the charity was attempting to tackle, one of the directors – a local journalist – took me on a walking tour of the area around the hostel in the early evening. I knew I had bitten off more than I could chew when he loaded and then stuffed a pistol down his trousers as we left his apartment. In retrospect, it was probably way too dangerous a thing to do and in the following hour or so all the fears and anxieties I had felt before arriving were realised. Nothing prepared me for the brief but intense insight into a world I am ashamed to say I had never even considered before. It was to be one of the most eye-opening evenings of my life.

Over the next few hours, I saw at close quarters the plight of dozens of very young children whose lives are defiled by crime, drugs and appalling abuse. We walked for several blocks through ill-lit, litter-strewn streets with mostly boarded-up shops and storage units. The hostel takes in children who have been the victims of sexual violence and tries to rehabilitate them. Nearly all the children – boys and girls – had been raped, mostly it seemed by family members: brothers, fathers, uncles and grandfathers. A great many were HIV-positive, working as prostitutes, and were addicted to a cocaine by-product called *basuko*. This they placed in a plastic drinks bottle, mixed with gasoline, and hung it around their necks on a string so they could sniff it near-constantly.

Some were tiny, as young as ten years old, and made even

smaller than normal through long-term malnutrition. Many of the young teenage girls were already mothers. At the hostel, they were given medical and psychological treatment and, if they stayed, they were taught some kind of trade: car mechanics, circus skills or hairdressing. On the way to the hostel, we stopped to look at posters that had been put up on the side of buildings by local vigilantes, keen to remove the children from their neighbourhood. The posters were advertising the forthcoming funerals of actual living kids in an attempt to warn them off the streets. By this stage, the physical fear that I had felt earlier in the evening had been numbed. I was in shock.

Just when I thought this experience could not get any more bizarre, we met a young girl called Claudia. Claudia had spent time in the hostel but had been asked to leave for repeated drug-taking. This is tough love: the rules on abstinence are strict. She was now back on the streets. Claudia looked at me oddly and said something I could not understand in Spanish. My friend laughed and translated. She had been partly trained as a hairdresser and she was asking who on earth cut my hair. She went on to explain to me that my hair was, in effect, on back to front, that the curly wispy bits should be at the front and the thick clumpy bit at the back. Previously, I had paid little attention to how my hair was cut. I kept it short and side-parted to stop it sticking up on end but otherwise it was stylistically unremarkable, and no doubt dull. But it evidently violated Claudia's aesthetic sense. She seemed outraged that more care had not been taken in trying to overcome these genetic deficiencies through better styling. As we left her, we encouraged her to return to the hostel. But she was still indignant that a barber in New York was providing inferior haircuts that fell well below her high standards.

The next morning, my mind still reeling from what I had seen the night before, I set off to figure out how to help my client – an investment fund – get out of its predicament. It was a struggle to change gear, to be back on the corporate track and apply myself to the tribulations of a big international company, when my head was filled with the heart-wrenching exposure I had experienced among the almost forgotten street kids down the road.

It was one of those problems that in retrospect seems so bizarre but is the logical consequence of doing business in unfamiliar geographies. You can encounter similar problems in London, Glasgow, Boston or Los Angeles if you do not know what you are doing. But this particular problem was in Colombia's second city, Medellín. It gave this situation an atmosphere of malice and extreme jeopardy. When I discovered the details of exactly what kind of pickle they had got themselves into, my first instinct was to head back to the airport and return immediately to New York. But the extraordinary events of the night before and my brief encounter with the depraved underbelly of Bogotá gave me something approaching resolve, or at least it had left me so dumbstruck I could not think of an excuse quickly enough as to why I needed to go home and hide under the bed.

Our client had bought an ice-cream business. Not a bad idea in Medellín, located near the equator with a population close to three million people, nearly all of whom enjoy a *helado* whenever possible. The problem was this was not only an ice-cream business. It had been infiltrated by the Medellín cartel. Even though the cartel's erstwhile leader, Pablo Escobar, had been killed a couple of years earlier, it was still in the business of producing large quantities of cocaine.

The cartel had devised an ingenious scheme to

simultaneously disperse part of the production process (thereby reducing the possibility of detection by the authorities) and also create employment and dependency among the local community. Each morning a fleet of vans would leave the factory to deliver ice cream to shops, cafés, restaurants and kiosks around the city. The same vans would also deliver partly processed cocaine paste to young mothers stuck indoors all day with small children and old people with similarly limited mobility. This population – young and old – would then spend the day slowly crystallising the paste by hand, mostly using hairdryers. The vans would return to the various legitimate vendors in the evening to collect the empty ice-cream containers but also stop off to pick up the now partially crystallised cocaine.

It was genius. Whoever devised the scheme should have been teaching at Harvard Business School. It reduced employment costs, factory overheads and the security bill as well as fulfilling their community obligations – all at the same time. It meant they could dominate the local market by offering ice cream at lower prices than their rivals because the highly profitable cocaine business acted as a subsidy to the mint chocolate chip, rum and raisin and raspberry ripple.

As well as being genius it was also highly illegal, immoral and brought our unwitting client into intimate contact with one of the most unpleasant organisations in the world. When they had tried to alter the production and distribution systems, bombs had gone off in the factory and government investigators had been shot. Figuring out a solution was, not surprisingly, quite tricky. Problems like this are like a virus that attack the body. There are things you can do to alleviate the symptoms but only time, often a course of bitter medicine, and an altered lifestyle will correct the underlying malaise.

In this case, the company was lucky. The local governor who would later become president had got much tougher on tackling the power of the cartel. For once, they were swimming with the tide of history.

But there was no quick fix. Time and again this can be the hardest advice to convey. Many senior executives have *Type A* personalities. They want rapid resolution and prefer immediate action to long-term strategies that patiently unravel a delicate problem and put in place the prophylactic measures needed for mitigation. *Muddling through* is a tricky solution to sell to scared, stressed people but it is often the only realistic option. They certainly do not like being told that they may be making the situation worse. On many occasions, it has fallen to me as an outsider to break bad news to senior bosses on the basis that telling truth to power is easier if you are not part of the internal management structure. That mostly holds true, but it is also sometimes the case that the easiest thing to do is to shoot the messenger. I have left many client offices over the years, figuratively at least, riddled with bullet holes.

I remember explaining to a US-based investor why his Colombian hydroelectric power plant was losing money. It was not, as he had been told by his underlings, because of freak weather conditions caused by El Niño. They had come up with detailed studies showing how water levels in Colombia's mighty Magdalena River were being adversely affected by unusual weather systems and drier than expected conditions. In truth, the local management had tried to cut costs by hiring illegal Venezuelan labour. These workers had triggered a massive brawl and punch-up in the nearby town, causing the plant to be blockaded by angry locals, who then set fire to the general manager's house. No work had been done for months. I had to painstakingly explain to him that

I was telling him this because it was true and not because I wanted to ruin his day. I think he believed me.

Cases like this leave you wondering how smart people ever get themselves into such pickles in the first place – buying companies where they do not really know how the money is made, or investing millions, often with little knowledge of what is actually happening on the ground. It seems crazy. Surely, they should have been able to figure out some of this in advance and dodge the problems that then beset them?

But it happens too often for it to be a simple case of human ineptitude. Something else happens when people make bad decisions. Very often there is a kind of collective cognitive dissonance at work. People are party to decisions that they publicly support but privately disagree with. The tendency is for groups – particularly those mostly comprised of men gripped by groupthink – to gravitate towards a positive decision and to suppress their concerns. Most people in competitive environments do not want to come across as being excessively timorous. They want to be seen to be bold and ambitious. And when several people are involved in the decision, then they wrongly assume that someone else has the answers to the questions that have been privately troubling them. It is why so often unanimously agreed decisions do not get implemented. Everybody appears to be supportive and committed, but in fact they have no intention of doing what they just said they would. In the passive-aggressive world of corporate decision-making, *agree, comply, evade* is very often what happens.

It is easy to be wise after the event. And the same people who said absolutely nothing at the time are often the most vociferous in explaining how they were not really ever convinced. On many occasions, I have backed the wrong project or hired the wrong people. I have made some real whoppers. There is then nothing more irritating than when the mistake has been realised and you are full of contrition and someone pipes up and explains that he (it usually is) was never a believer in the first place. This is a great argument for gun control in the workplace. There are plenty of times when I would gladly have shot someone dead on the spot for being smugly wise after the event.

The ice cream case was to be my baptism by fire, and I found myself returning to Colombia many times over the years to help figure out a whole range of equally odd situations. Perhaps the most unusual involved a client whose oil installations in guerrilla-occupied territory were being repeatedly blown up. Colombia's oil industry is often located in hostile territory in parts of the country effectively controlled by guerrillas or other paramilitary groups who have for years kidnapped oil workers. I once debriefed a British executive who had been kidnapped by guerrillas in this part of Colombia and held in a series of jungle camps for months on end. I asked him what the conditions had been like during his captivity. 'Not too bad,' he explained. 'Essentially, you just had to endure bad food, long walks in near-constant rain, extended periods of boredom, occasional outbreaks of random violence and the persistent possibility of sodomy. In fact, pretty much identical to being at a Scottish boarding school in the 1950s.'

The engineering in Colombia is complicated by the geology: they often have to drill horizontally under the Andes to get to the oil. Working these fields and staying safe is not for beginners. The oil and gas sector has long been the target of choice for anybody with a grudge against the government or big business operating in the country. But what was to unfold on this occasion was unusual even by the mind-warping standards of back-woods Colombia.

Our client was bringing a lawsuit against the financial backers of the project. To do so, they needed to be able to demonstrate that the level of attacks they were now experiencing had increased markedly due to a change of tactics by the local insurgents away from common harassment to a deliberate strategy of putting them out of business. As part of preparing their case, our client needed to be able to pinpoint the moment at which the decision was taken to switch bombing tactics and why. Our client's lawyers wanted a detailed assessment undertaken of how the bombing campaign had been planned and orchestrated.

I have worked with hundreds of lawyers over the years. Some of my best friends and relations are lawyers. I think in the main they do a very good and valuable job. Could the world do with fewer of them? Probably – and a judicious cull would no doubt be appropriate. But by and large I am all in favour of the profession.

There is one sub-species of attorney, however, that I try to avoid whenever possible: the attack dog. The kind of snarling, street-fighting lawyer whom you let off the leash when you are in a tight corner and you cannot afford to take any prisoners. In this case, the lawyer was not an attack dog but an attack werewolf whose veins, it seemed, had been drained and the blood replaced by weapons-grade pure testosterone laced with radioactive isotopes. And who had developed a disregard for fundamental human dignity that would make the most hardened commandant of a North Korean concentration camp write in protest to Amnesty International.

That she was a woman, I know, should not matter. But somehow it did. I was terrified of her. Nothing we did pleased her. We profiled all the insurgent groups in the area, drew timelines and made charts and graphs of every conceivable type. We explained with extraordinary granularity what had been going on. All we got in return was a lip-curling sneer and a refusal to pay our bills. And then we hit the jackpot.

Through somebody who knew somebody who knew somebody else, we found the explosives expert from the insurgent group who had been instrumental not just in the bombing campaign but who had been present when the group decided to change tactics. He had been captured on the battlefield. Through a government amnesty programme, he had served a greatly reduced prison term, provided intelligence and been released with a new identity on supervised parole. We met him and he agreed to testify for our client.

Our client might as well have had the muscles in her cheek which enable the formation of a smile surgically removed. I never saw her look anything approaching happy or pleased. But when we told her who we had recruited to the team, she briefly stopped shouting at us and paid one of our invoices. We interpreted that as her being deliriously grateful. She should have been. A hopeless case had suddenly got half a chance of success. But he was weird. He spoke little English but the small amount he did speak, he spoke with a distinct Northern Irish accent. He had been instructed in the use of Semtex explosive by a visiting training team from the IRA, which added a surreal quality to our conversations. At the time, the Colombian insurgent groups were trading expertise with various other groups around the world. How he would come across over a video link to a court in the US was anybody's guess. But for now, that was the least of our problems.

His recreational activities were in ascending order of enjoyment: getting whip-snortingly drunk; riding his motorbike at high speed at night with no lights on; taking industrial quantities of cocaine; and sleeping with the wives of his former guerrilla colleagues who were away fighting the government in the jungle. Ideally, he liked to undertake all of these activities simultaneously. Our problem was less whether an American judge would understand his Hispanic take on an Ulster dialect and more how we were going to keep him alive.

Multiply the probability of him dying from alcohol poisoning by the chance of him being killed in a traffic accident, by the likelihood of him suffering a fatal drug overdose, by the near certainty of him coming to a sticky end in a brutal revenge killing, and our odds of delivering him on the day were vanishingly small. And to add one further complication, the security detail who were looking after him loathed him. They had all formerly served in the Colombian military and were not sympathetic to their former adversary. To put it mildly.

And then the case settled out of court. There would be no trial; it was all over, and we went our separate ways. Our client was heartbroken. Not because it was not a lucrative result for her and her client; far from it. But she had obviously been looking forward to the big scrap, to dismembering the opposition legal team and then dragging their limbless corpses back to her lair as macabre trophies. Like a boxer who is primed and ready for combat, high on adrenaline, only to be told that the fight is cancelled at the moment he climbs into the ring. By contrast, I was thrilled. It had been the strangest of times, and one that is much more agreeable and amusing to write down years later than it was to live through.

If these were formative times for me, then they were extraordinary times for Colombia. My experiences were set against the backdrop of a country going through profound transition – a two-decade shift from the brink of state failure to becoming a nation that has a fighting chance of realising a good proportion of its enormous potential. It has taken risks for peace. Internal civil conflicts – from Ireland to South Africa – nearly always end with sworn enemies breaking bread together. Enemies who have spent years inflicting terrible and cruel suffering both on each other – and many innocent bystanders – eventually find a different kind of courage and sit down and negotiate a way out. That has been the story of the Colombian peace process. For many, talking to terrorists can never be condoned or forgiven. It will always be a betrayal that grinds salt into raw, deep wounds that will never heal. But most often it is the only way forward. Many people in the UK found it hard to stomach Queen Elizabeth shaking hands with the former IRA commander-turned Sinn Fein politician, Martin McGuiness. But it is how peace is made.

Courage alone is never enough. Serendipity plays a part as well. In Colombia's case, the end of the Cold War changed the ideological context and material support for left-wing revolutionaries. At a more local level, it needed a tough if controversial new president, Alvaro Uribe, who had earned his spurs fighting the cartels, to break the complacency. It also needed a US administration that backed him, morally and militarily. It is often unfashionable, particularly in Latin America, to think that anything good can come from what people still see as Yankee imperialism. But the plain fact is that on this occasion it was decisive. This is not to absolve the US from the many mistakes they made over the years, and it was of course the insatiable appetite of middle-class America to snort white powder up their noses that fuelled and financed so much of the conflict in the first place.

I met President Uribe on several occasions. He is an unusual politician. No doubt part of him is motivated by the same narcissistic tendency that drives most politicians, but he seems different from many of the others I have met. He is, in effect, a single-issue politician. He has been mayor of Medellín, governor of Antioquia, a senator and then president from 2002 to 2010. Consistently, he has been driven by the burning desire to defeat the guerrilla groups that have fought the government for years and killed his father in 1983. Along the way, he also played his part in breaking the power of the cartels. He is controversial, and allegations of links to far-right paramilitaries have dogged him for years, as has the human rights record of Colombian military units engaged in the war against the guerrillas. In person, he is polite and intense. He listens carefully to what you say, which does not mean he agrees with you or is willing to change his mind. He rarely does. But he is accessible and willing to talk for hours. No doubt, he is dogmatic, stubborn and willing to take risks to get what he wants. But he is a rare example of a political leader driven not simply by vanity, personal aggrandisement or the pursuit of power for power's sake, but by the tunnelled, single-minded conviction that he and his cause are right.

The passage of time always helps in the pursuit of peace. After forty years of conflict, the leaders of the armed groups that fought the government grew old. As young men and women, living in a rain-sodden jungle with its impossible vertiginous terrain was a hardship worth bearing. But as the decades passed, the cause was corrupted, the justification harder to defend and the leadership grew aged and weary. When the opportunity came, they were ready to make peace. The revolution ran out of revolutionaries.

Colombia gets under your skin. It is not unique in that, of course. But like many others, I have been beguiled by the country over the quarter of a century I have been going there. It is a breathtakingly beautiful and intriguing place. I think often of the strange situations I have found myself in with clients who have conspired to get themselves into the strangest of dilemmas. I think too of fantastic nights out, smoking cigars and drinking the local liquor, *aguardiente*, sitting on the old city walls looking out to sea in Cartagena, the jewel of a city on Colombia's Caribbean coast. But I think more often of that young girl, Claudia, alone on the mean streets of Bogotá and I hope that at least some of Colombia's new-found good fortune trickles down to her.

6

Porn, corn and paranoia

IMMIGRATION OFFICIALS at airports always give me the willies. There is something about handing over my passport to someone of stern countenance wearing a uniform that makes me assume the demeanour of a first-time drug smuggler. My heart rate accelerates, my palms sweat, and I walk awkwardly, in the ungainly manner of someone with a rectum full of heroin.

Authority induces guilt in me even when I have nothing to be guilty about. And the longer the immigration queue to enter a country, the guiltier I will behave by the time I get to the front of the line and hand over my documents. Once, entering the United States through Miami International Airport, I was questioned by an immigration officer who had the world-weary look of someone who had heard every fanciful story under the sun and not believed any of them. By the time I took my turn in front of her, I was already sweating badly and had an uncontrollable urge to fidget repeatedly with my bottom, rather like the tennis player Rafael Nadal fiddling with his crack on match-point. She looked at me with evident disdain, as if she had already decided that I was exactly the kind of undesirable the United States did not need to admit. When she asked me why I had so many entry stamps in my passport from Colombia, Venezuela, Panama, Nigeria and Afghanistan – *'this ain't looking good, boy'* – I was almost ready to confess to a long career in the global narcotics trade.

I checked myself just in time and started trying to explain why a job in international security required regular trips to such places. Unfortunately, when I opened my mouth to speak, rather than my usual trusty baritone, I sounded like one of the castrati from the Sistine Chapel Choir. An odd combination of boredom and anxiety induced a high-pitched soprano squeak sufficient for her to dispatch me for secondary questioning forthwith.

Entering Russia through Sheremetyevo Airport also brings out my inherent shiftiness. Nowadays the airport has the veneer of business-like efficiency. But back in the early 1990s, the whole place was a microcosm of the disjuncture between the end of the Soviet Union and the onset of rampant cowboy capitalism. The terminal building was designed to cope with the very small number of Russians permitted to travel and the similarly limited number of foreigners able to visit Russia in the late 1950s. It certainly was not designed to cope with the flood of ravenous bankers and businesspeople that descended on the country in the immediate aftermath of the collapse of the USSR. By the early Nineties, the great sell-off of national assets was underway, as the new Russian government attempted to privatise their way out of the economic catastrophe that had precipitated the demise of the mighty Soviet empire.

Western money came pouring in, and with it a hotchpotch of foreign investors. A few would go on to make fortunes, most would scuttle back home to safer climes in Frankfurt, New York, Zurich or London when they realised the harsh realities of doing business in this new version of Russia. But for now, there was a heady confidence that Russia would rapidly adjust to the norms of European business and while it did, there was money to be made. I was among those nursing such hopes. I arrived for the first time in Russia as we set about establishing an office to service the growing sense among investors that this was going to be trickier than they first thought. That Russia's new entrepreneur class was making up the rules to suit itself as it went along.

This is why I found myself, one freezing February morning, handing over my passport and immigration form to one of the most extraordinary-looking women I had ever seen. She was svelte in a way that her Miami counterpart was not. But any hint of Slavic sensuality was offset by what seemed like inch-deep make-up caked on her face. It was like the cement they use to line the inside of nuclear reactors. This gave her a waxen, lifeless quality that made me wonder if on her days off she occasionally acted as a body-double in Lenin's mausoleum. She stared impassively over my left shoulder (she was not the first woman to do that). This was either because she was bored out of her mind or more likely because her hair was tied back so tautly under her peaked military cap that, when combined with the atomic-proof foundation on her face, a form of premature rigor mortis had actually set in.

When my time came, I stepped forward and handed over my documents. This time I was anxious for good reason. In addition to my normal airport-induced angst, I had 20,000 US dollars stuffed down the front of my trousers. The Soviet-era banking system had still not caught up with the needs of foreign start-ups and, for now, cash was king. On this occasion, my job was to bring in the working capital our fledgeling operation needed to pay the wages. For once, my stiff-legged gait was authentic, caused by the way a tightly rolled wedge of cash was acting as a ligature in my groin. I was worried that the immigration official would assume wrongly that I had a condom stuffed full of pharmaceutical contraband cached in my lower intestine. I tried to play it cool and flashed what I hoped was a winning smile at the immobile mannequin on the other side of the glass screen. Not a flicker.

It got worse. As I handed over my travel documents, I realised to my horror that I must have had a mental spasm when completing the immigration form. On the section that asked you to state whether or not you had any firearms, drugs or works of art, I had ticked yes rather than no. I spotted my error just when it was too late to grab back the form and correct it. My already sky-high blood pressure rocketed, and I stood there waiting to be taken away, searched, interrogated and dispatched to a lifetime in the gulag.

But no. After what seemed like an eternity of her staring past me blankly into space, she stamped my passport and slid it back to me across her desk. Either she had seen the mistake, realised I was an idiot and let it go or, more likely, she had long since stopped any vague pretence at doing her job and was merely going through the motions in this stupor of bureaucratic ennui. I did not wait to find out. I mumbled my gratitude, picked up my bag and walked as fast as I could to the exit. The doors opened and I was met by an icy blast of frigid Russian air so cold that I feared it would freeze the bogies in my nose.

That first visit in the heart of a freezing Russian winter was not the start of my fascination with the country. I had studied the Russian Revolution, been taught the Soviet political system and learned of the sacrifices made in the defeat of Napoleon and then Nazism. More vividly, I had sat bolt upright in open-mouthed amazement when I first saw Julie Christie on screen playing Lara in the film version of *Doctor Zhivago*. My already supercharged teen hormones were sent into frenzied overdrive with the revelation that such sublime feminine beauty could be manifest in human form. The fact that she did not look remotely Russian and that her accent was woeful were irrelevant details. I felt I had glimpsed the erotic mystique of the Russian soul. And I liked it.

After searching Moscow unsuccessfully for any sign of Ms Christie, I turned my mind to trying to figure out what was going on in this vast country I had read so much about. Not surprisingly, it has proved a complex and never-ending task. Over the years, I have been many times, trying to help clients grappling with all manner of issues. As the decades have ticked by, I have become preoccupied by trying to understand why, in the space of a few decades, Russia would go full circle, from cold-war nuclear-armed enemy to hot new emerging market and then back to hostile geo-political and military rival.

That we should be surprised is, in one sense, the consequence of a well-worn pattern of investor behaviour whereby new markets get horribly over-hyped. Politics can scupper the neat exponential economic growth predictions that cause opportunity-hungry investors to salivate in anticipation at the rare chance to jump on the bandwagon of double-digit GDP growth. It happens the world over. Myanmar was set to be the flash new Asian tiger. In Aung San Suu Kyi, it had an internationally respected, photogenic and charismatic leader. She was the darling of the global liberal elite, adorned with the Nobel prize and multiple honorary doctorates from the world's top universities. She had made great personal sacrifices to take a stand for her people. And then Burmese nationalism reared its ugly head and the Rohingya people were chased out of town. Aung San Suu Kyi suddenly looked less like Asia's answer to Nelson Mandela and more like any other politician with feet of clay. Similarly, Iran seemed to be inching its way to some kind of rapprochement with the West, signing a deal to restrict its nuclear ambitions with the Obama administration and the European Union. Investors were eyeing its vast hydrocarbon reserves and youthful population lasciviously. And then President Trump turned up and the party was abruptly cancelled.

Some of what happened in Russia can be explained by that familiar trend: wide-eyed investors and their enablers in the investment banking community peddling gateway drugs that skew the upside data and suppress any inconvenient truths. Reality then dawns, fair-weather funds grumble and take their money elsewhere, leaving the field for the more savvy, battle-hardened, less squeamish investors to take a more nuanced punt on markets that will always throw up more than their fair share of surprises.

But Russia's story is more than one of over-enthusiastic naiveté being ratcheted back in the face of sober reality. What puzzles me most about Russia is the rival and diametrically opposite interpretations of why the country behaves as it does. Different people take the same data and arrive at wildly different conclusions. This is most graphically captured in how people see Mikhail Gorbachev. For many in the West, he was and still is the brave proto-democrat who called out the inevitable failings of a corrupted and corroded system, a patriot who realised the game was up and tried to steer Russia to safer waters but was undone by the reactionary forces of the Russian establishment. By contrast, most Russians think he sold them down the river. Indeed, most of my otherwise liberal Russian friends see him as a weakling who spinelessly betrayed Mother Russia and the Soviet Union to a treacherous West. I have no doubt that both assessments of Gorbachev – hero or villain – are wrong, but the space between the two extreme views was just the beginning of a fissure that has only deepened over time.

For a while though, it seemed, at least from outside Russia, that there was some consensus on where the country might be heading. That Russia might become like Germany, another country that used to go around invading its neighbours but swapped territorial aggression for manufacturing superb motor cars and not spending very much on defence. Indeed, the Russian government in the early 1990s was making all the right noises, scripted by a phalanx of advisers from Harvard University preaching a free-market creed with evangelical fervour. This early optimism proved a false dawn. The history of Russia since has been one of these two widely differing interpretations. Either it is the story of a mendacious and duplicitous West, peddling snake-oil economics, stealthily plotting the expansion of NATO and the EU while intent on driving the final nail into Russia's cold-war coffin. Or it is a tale of well-intentioned and competent reformers supported by the magnanimity of the West being muscled out of the way by an oligarch class set upon the daylight robbery of Russia's national assets for their own selfish ends.

With the turn of the millennium, the two narratives diverge further. The arrival of President Putin is seen by many as the salvation of Russia, the restorer of prestige who stands up to the US and makes Russia relevant again. Someone who gives the Russian people the stability and status they regard as their birthright. For others – and this is the narrative that dominates in the West – he is the KGB hard man, a *racketeer with rockets*, as he has been called, who has entrenched the seizure of the country's wealth in the hands of a gang of hard-nosed cronies while ruthlessly repurposing the apparatus of the state to undermine democracy and stability. And not just in Russia's own backyard in Ukraine and Georgia but right under the noses of electorates around the world.

This binary view of the same facts – victim or aggressor – is of course easy to grasp with a degree of hindsight. Back in the early 1990s, most of our clients did not have the luxury of this kind of perspective. Nor were they particularly interested in where we were in the grand arc of geo-politics. They were just trying to figure out what was going on at the coalface. And for many it was not pretty.

Back then, Russia could be rather scary. I remember being left alone in the office in Moscow one morning while my colleagues dispersed around the city to see clients in varying states of distress. After a while, the office door opened and an elderly lady – what the Russians call a babushka – whom I had seen in the building foyer earlier that morning popped her head around the door. She was followed by three burly men – unshaven and with shaved heads – who pushed past her into the office. They were wearing leather jackets over ill-fitting nylon tracksuits. One of them was carrying a large monkey wrench.

They started shouting at me. I assumed they were members of one of the criminal gangs that I had read so much about that brazenly menace and extort businesses in Moscow. They looked and sounded extremely threatening and insistent, as if I was about to be bundled into the back of a van and taken to some remote dacha outside the city. There I would be systematically tortured before my bloodied, dismembered corpse was discarded in a snowdrift, not to be discovered until the spring thaw.

At this point, just as I was about to fall to my knees and start praying to a god I didn't think I believed in (but was now urgently having second thoughts about), the door opened and one of my Russian-speaking colleagues returned. Accustomed to dealing with skinheads in tracksuits, he started shouting back at my three would-be abductors. Turning to me, he saw my ashen face and trembling knees. 'What's wrong with you?' he asked. I explained how we were both now facing imminent, probably fatal, peril. He burst out laughing. 'They are plumbers, you moron,' he explained. 'They're here to fix the toilet. They just want to know if you want to go to the loo before they turn the water off.'

Not all of our clients were as spineless as I am, and many of them faced genuine danger as they set up shop in Russia, in a state where the criminal grip on many commercial activities had been ingrained for decades. In 2015 I enjoyed a splendid Japanese dinner in the so-called House on the Embankment, a grand old apartment building on the river across from the Kremlin. Sometimes known as the House of Shadows, it is where government officials and their families were housed in the 1930s. During Stalin's purges over a third of its residents were alleged to have been taken away, either to prison or, more likely, for execution. From the upper stories, they would be able to see Stalin's secret police, the NKVD, arrive in a Black Raven, the standard-issue police vehicle, wondering if it was their turn to be taken away. It must have been a terrifying place. But that evening, all that menace felt like ancient history. Moscow felt like a modern international city, a feeling encouraged by copious amounts of expensive sake, washed down with even more expensive vodka and fine Georgian wine. After dinner that evening, we left the House on the Embankment and walked across the river towards the Kremlin. By the side of the road was an impromptu floral tribute to Boris Nemtsov, the opposition politician and democracy activist who had been shot dead a few days earlier by un-named assailants while walking home with his girlfriend.

It was a timely reminder. Central Moscow has had money lavished on it in the decades since the demise of the Soviet Union, particularly by long-term mayor Yuri Luzhkov, who was encouraged in this by President Putin, until they fell out. Both men were eager to deter Muscovites from taking to the streets by showering civic munificence on them. Moscow is not at all representative of Russia, but Putin, in particular, knows that it is where Russian revolutions tend to start. Behind the modernity and the restoration, Nemtsov's death was indicative that this is still a place where the exercise of power can be brutish. And leaving Russia for good is no guarantee of safety if you have fallen out of favour with the wrong people.

I always felt it seemed worse in the winter. Moscow winters are so harsh, dark and foreboding, even if they can also be exquisitely beautiful. It is easy to feel a sense of impending danger. By contrast, in the summer, Moscow feels like Stockholm – warm and light until late in the evening, with sensational restaurants, making it all the more difficult to set an accurate gauge of where this city sits in the Top Trumps league table of risky cities. Like the plumbers, Russians often sound murderous when they are at their most solicitous.

Appearances are more deceptive here than in most places. It is easy to suffer from widespread confirmation bias – the tendency to interpret new information as confirmation of your existing beliefs. I was once meeting an American client who ran a chain of movie theatres in Russia's most prominent cities. Like many investors who cross swords with Russia's real estate moguls, he had found that life had suddenly got complicated. We chatted for a while before he suggested he introduce me to one of his Russian suppliers.

We met in a hotel lobby. The supplier was dressed like a cowboy. Not a regular cow-lassoing cowboy – more like a leather-fetishist cowboy. He was dressed from head to toe, from wide-brimmed Texan-style hat to highly polished boots, in leather, all in various tones of black. He even had the big droopy Village People-style moustache. He was friendly enough and introduced me to his girlfriend. In stark contrast, her clothing choices were what you might call minimalist. She was sulky and supremely disinterested. She sat, semi-naked, chain-smoking sullenly while we talked. I asked what it was that he supplied.

'Porn', he explained matter-of-factly.

The conversation continued between him and my client as they discussed pricing models, customer demand and where next they were planning to extend the distribution network. Now I am as broad-minded as the next person, maybe more so. But on this occasion, my natural libertarianism deserted me. Instead, I felt the dour morality of my Methodist upbringing reasserting itself after a long absence. Having shaken his hand, I involuntarily wiped my palm on the back of my trousers. The meeting finished. We said goodbye to the porno-cowboy and his sidekick, whom I was now convinced was the star attraction of much of the merchandise. As we headed to the door, I broached the issue with my client as tactfully as I could. Was it wise, I asked, to be meeting a pornographer so publicly and were there any wider risks that we should discuss?

'Porn?' he exclaimed. 'No, you idiot. I said corn – he supplies all our popcorn.' Never judge a book by its leather-bound cover, particularly in Moscow.

Like most cities with a criminal edge, Russia in the 1990s did have a seedy underbelly that was to prove the undoing of many a client whose extra-curricular activities ended in, at best, shame and embarrassment or, at worst, compromise and extortion. Some found the siren's call of Moscow's promiscuous nightlife too much to resist, with hair-raising consequences. Indeed, back in the 1990s, a night out in Moscow would often conclude with a ride home in the most unlikely transportation. To try to make ends meet, private citizens – and often anybody with access to a vehicle – would moonlight as taxi drivers. I remember heading back to my hotel in a police car, an army truck and, on one surreal occasion, the back of an ambulance. Luckily, the on-board patient was not in a life-threatening condition and seemed happy enough for the company.

As the years have gone by and the street-fighting excesses of Russia's gangsters have been brought to heel, the issues our clients face have become less physically intimidating but more intractable. Yet, equally, their level of sophistication and ability to navigate around the mantraps has improved immeasurably. The early optimists, high on the simple narcotic of Russia's rapid transition to democratic capitalism, have long-since departed. Those that are left generally have the guile to survive and prosper even if the local management often feels at odds with its bosses at corporate headquarters over which version of Russia they have placed their faith in.

But it is not all plain sailing. I recall a conversation with a partner from a smart British law firm who sat in my office in London recounting a predicament that his client had managed to get themselves into. It sounded like the script of an espionage thriller. A massive illegal oil trade orchestrated in the upper reaches of the Kremlin that was financed by the Vatican, involving Israeli intelligence and Chechen mobsters. It all sounded so far-fetched it was likely that much of it had been fabricated to deter him and his client from trying to enforce a contract. I did my best to reassure him and help him find the elusive point at which he was robustly defending his client's interests but without putting himself or them in undue danger.

He felt acutely vulnerable. It was if he had strayed too close to the edge of a cliff and he could feel the ground slipping under him. My job was to grab his hand and pull him back. Over several meetings we talked about all the different scenarios of what may happen. The process of talking it all through in itself offered him some reassurance, as did the realisation that he had options, that he was not just at the mercy of capricious fate. He relaxed a little. But as he left my office to take the train home to leafy Surrey, he still looked a troubled man. Russia – for the uninitiated – can do that to you.

My lawyer friend's predicament was a useful reminder that Russia's story is intimately entwined with its great natural resource: oil, or to be more accurate, its carbon cousin, gas. It was the precipitous decline in the oil price in the early 1980s that rang the death knell for the Soviet Union. Trying to match the US in military spending while bearing the formidable cost of invading Afghanistan proved too much when the main artery of its already sclerotic economy suddenly contracted.

Conversely, the revival of the oil price from the late 1990s onwards, gave the Russian economy an adrenaline shot to the heart sufficient for the country to regain some of its old swagger.

As Russia's hydrocarbon industry has become more efficient and productive, with the help of foreign capital and technology, the country has become more resilient to the vagaries of the international oil price and more assertive in determining how that price is set. Oil remains the circulatory system on which Russia's prosperity depends. Hydrocarbons are like economic embalming fluid – they can ensure that parts of your economy that have long since died maintain the appearance of being alive. And during the booms, it can inoculate the country – as it has in Russia – against the need for reform and diversification. For sure, Russia has some world-class treasury planners and central bankers that keep the show on the road; it is not the economic basket-case many of its detractors would claim. But oil and gas, its greatest assets, remain also its Achilles heel.

Which of these versions of Russia is the authentic reality? Is it the once great nation that gave the world Tolstoy, Tchaikovsky and Dostoevsky, put the first man into space and has produced some of the greatest scientific brains in the world? A defiant people who will suffer loss and hardship on a scale intolerable elsewhere to defend their homeland from foreign aggression? Napoleon and Hitler both thought victory was theirs until Russian resistance and the ferocious cold sent them packing. A country that, since the end of the Cold War, has been the victim of a grand conspiracy? When it was at its most vulnerable, it was starved of the funds that were readily available to other countries. It then had to endure the embarrassment of the Yeltsin years before it found a way to recover its self-respect. Is it a country that has had to resort to a more assertive foreign policy only in the face of pernicious meddling by the United States, military expansionism from NATO and economic imperialism from the European Union? If America does not like some of what Russia is prepared to do – its sophisticated use of asymmetric cyber warfare and news manipulation, for instance – when its interests are at risk, then it is guilty of the grossest hypocrisy. And if you do not like what Russia has done in Ukraine or Syria then think what the West has done in Central America, Iraq, Afghanistan, Libya and elsewhere. This is a version of recent history – however incoherent or biased it may sound to a Western ear – that many Russians would sign up to. Maybe not all of it, and I suspect many Russians do not like the tone, style and greed of some of their leaders, but in essence they see themselves in Shakespearean terms as more sinned against than sinning.

Or is this just the propaganda spin-machine in the Kremlin working overtime? The other reality is that the Russian state was captured long ago by an elite that has used its oil and other wealth to medicate enough of the population into compliance. A gilded, opulent elite, where the senior cadre of politicians and their billionaire banker and industrial counterparts are co-beneficiaries in the same grand scam designed for their own preservation. Where the longevity of a regime that lives in a bubble of its own conceit has decided that the normal rules do not apply to them and they will do almost anything, both at home and abroad, with little concern for morality or international decency to further their own interests.

I am not sure what to believe – or which bits of which argument have greater credence. I have listened to too many German automakers, Italian agriculturists and French industrialists arguing for a relaxation of Russian trade sanctions not to be able to spot the limitations of their naked self-interest. And I have heard how pompous and myopic Western politicians can sound when pontificating on Russia. What is indisputable is that the Russian leadership is wily and cunning. They are some of the most effective political knife-fighters around, with a detached, deeply pragmatic, clear-eyed realism. As one of the characters in the US mafia series, *The Sopranos*, explains, Americans are unable to imagine the worst ever happening while Russians know for certain that it will.

The Russian people do not have infinite patience, even if it stretches much further than their counterparts in the West. At some stage, they may tire of stunted opportunities and an economy that lacks the diversity, verve and flexibility to deliver opportunities. They may no longer be willing to accept the same dish of reheated nationalism and victimhood without something more positive to inspire confidence in the future. The Russian state may ultimately be undone by its own lack of imagination. This journey of exploration continues. Trying to define what makes Russia tick seems like a journey without end. On one level, Russia has changed so much since that first visit of mine. But while it is radically different, it is also stubbornly the same, not least in the way that Russia and the West find it so difficult to reach any kind of shared understanding, finding it easier to blame each other than seek common ground. I wish it were different.

What would my impassive friend, the immigration officer at Sheremetyevo Airport, make of what has happened to her country in the last three decades? The airport has certainly had a facelift. The Border Service is now a subsidiary of the FSB, the successor to the KGB, and border guards now tend to be young, efficient and professional. There is even a number to call if you wish to complain, if you feel your immigration experience has been in some way sub-standard. I suspect they do not get many callers. Maybe she has retired, living the sedate life of a babushka in a crumbling apartment on her stretched state pension, nervous of what austerity reforms the government may introduce next time the oil price crashes. Perhaps she managed to quit the immigration service and re-invent herself in the new Russia. It is possible that she discovered a well-hidden passion for customer service. If so, she might be working at the elegant Café Pushkin in central Moscow, serving blinchiki, black caviar and borscht to Chinese businessmen, in town to negotiate some central Asian gas deal.

Actually, I have an inkling that she, like thousands of her compatriots, decided she could not face another snot-freezing Moscow winter and emigrated to Southern Florida, to Sunny Isles Beach – the suburb of choice for the Russian diaspora. She may now be working at Miami International Airport, as stony-faced and sphinx-like as ever. She will have fitted in well.

7

Driving with the handbrake on

'RIGHT. YOU HAVE TO WEAR THIS.'

   'No way. I am not putting that on.'

   'You've got to.'

   'I am not.'

   'You must.'

   'Fuck off.'

How on earth did I find myself having this argument? I was sitting in the back of a taxi late at night in a dark, unlit backstreet. Next to me was a Scottish lawyer intent on making me wear a blindfold. He was called Danny. This was not some macabre sexual role-play but apparently a necessary precondition for our clandestine mission that evening. We were on our way to visit the home of a retired Brazilian army officer, turned private detective. My Scottish companion had got it into his head that I needed to be blindfolded so that I would not know the location of where we were heading. Given that I had no idea where we were, did not want to be there in the first place, was regretting ever agreeing to come on such a stupid trip and had absolutely no intention of ever repeating the experience, I was adamant that I was not going to put his over-cologned scarf around my head.

We eventually agreed that I would not wear the blindfold in exchange for a solemn but pointless promise not to reveal the address of our destination. Since I didn't know it, I was happy to do so. A few minutes later, we pulled up outside a nondescript residential home in an equally anonymous-looking suburb. We got out of the taxi and rang the bell by the hefty steel gate that separated the small front garden from the street.

Nothing happened; nobody came. I breathed a sigh of relief and suggested we must have the wrong address. I was preparing to head back to my hotel when the gate was opened from the inside by a smart young man wearing pressed chinos and a polo shirt. He indicated that we should follow him. He took us around the side of the house, down a passageway and through another heavily fortified gate into a small walled garden in which stood a single-storey building with a light on inside. A ramp led up to a double set of French windows. Our guide told us to wait while he went up the ramp and inside. A few moments later he returned and gestured to us to follow him.

Inside, the building had been equipped as a standard executive office. As we entered, I noticed three, slightly older but equally smartly dressed men, each obviously in good physical shape, with short-cropped hair and athletic builds. They stood up, leaving the principal occupant of the room centre-stage in his wheelchair in front of me. He was painfully thin but sitting ramrod straight in his chair. His cadaverous face, pock-marked skin and unblinking eyes fixed me with a steady, unsmiling stare that unnerved me.

'Good evening Mr. Fenning. What a pleasure it is to meet you at last,' he said in fluent but heavily accented English. Instinctively, I stepped forward to shake hands only to realise that his arms were almost entirely paralysed. Seemingly, he could only use the fingers on his right hand to operate the controls of the electric wheelchair. 'Do not be embarrassed, please sit down.' He gestured towards a leather sofa in front of him. I heard the sound of the bolt as the French windows were locked.

I was in a scene from a James Bond movie. But rather than being dressed suavely in a tuxedo with a beautiful woman by my side and a Walther PPK tucked discreetly inside my jacket, I was wearing an ill-fitting suit and carrying an asthma inhaler. Rather than a glamorous Bond girl, I was accompanied by an amiable Scotsman, but one with a dangerous Walter Mitty complex. I felt sick.

Danny had persuaded me that this evening's assignment was our last chance to find a solution for a client with a particularly knotty problem. A European industrial company had been in Brazil for the longest time. New management at head office had conducted a review of their international operations and discovered that their Brazil business was not as unprofitable as they first thought. It was in fact making tons of money. But a large chunk of the profits was being siphoned off by the local management and their Brazilian partners. Further investigation revealed that their local partners were in cahoots with a particularly ruthless crime syndicate. Danny – an attorney and long-term resident of Brazil – had been advising them and, having decided he needed additional help, had asked me to see what we could do to try to turn things around. Once we realised the scale of the problem, Danny had suggested we seek assistance from the man sitting across from me, known only as '*O Coronel*' – The Colonel. Reluctantly, I had agreed to an exploratory meeting.

I was inexperienced, naive and new to Brazil, which is why I had grudgingly agreed to meet *O Coronel*. Now every fibre of my being was telling me this was a stupid idea, and we should get out of there as quickly as possible. But it was not that easy. These kinds of situations are quite intimidating. Theoretically, I was free to stand up, say that there had been an awful misunderstanding, apologise and leave. But in practice, I found myself rooted to the spot, unable to do anything other than listen to Danny – whose risk-radar had ceased functioning years before and who was revelling in the cloak-and-dagger menace of the conversation – explain our problem. Eventually, I summoned sufficient fortitude to cut in and try to bring matters to a head by asking our host how he felt he might be of assistance.

'I think this situation requires special measures,' *O Coronel* explained coldly. 'It will necessitate the deployment of our more traditional methodology. This we will do for your client.' He exuded malice. That was enough. I was not sure exactly what he was referring to but given that he and his associates had all served in the notorious intelligence wing of the former military dictatorship, I did not want to hang around to find out. I mumbled something about needing time to reflect and consult with my client. I stood up and steered a very reluctant Danny to the door and back to the sanctuary of my hotel.

That evening excursion was a very useful lesson. In choosing a career in security and intelligence, you open the door to a netherworld of fantasists, scoundrels and oddballs, many operating beyond the pale of acceptability. They all need to be kept at bay. Experiences like my brush with *O*

Coronel are essential in making you understand where the boundaries lie between what is ethical and acceptable and what is clearly not. It is one thing to understand this distinction cerebrally, and of course you can and should read it in a corporate governance manual. But it helps to also understand it viscerally – by scaring yourself half to death on a nocturnal jaunt with an over-enthusiastic Scotsman.

This is a side of Rio that few visitors see, thank goodness. Instead, the city is rightly famous for its wonderful beaches, extraordinary topography, iconic landmarks and carnival atmosphere. It is a city of sunshine with the occasional dark cloud. On one of my first visits, I was asked to speak at a chamber of commerce dinner held in one of Rio's swanky beachfront hotels. I arrived slightly late and had rushed by foot to get there as my taxi had been caught in traffic. I had opted to abandon the cab and cover the last 400 metres to the hotel at a light jog. I was wearing a wool suit with the thermal qualities required for a New York winter not a tropical Brazilian summer. By the time I emerged through the revolving doors into the hotel lobby, I was lathered-up like a jittery thorough-bred racehorse under starters' orders. Never a good look.

The evening's dinner was sponsored by a prominent brand of Scottish whisky and I was scheduled to deliver some pithy and insightful remarks on the state of the world after the chamber's guests had finished their main course. The whisky was flowing freely. But I made a firm decision that I was going to stick to my usual rule and not drink anything alcoholic until after I had delivered my remarks, when I could then relax properly. In any event, a whisky is not what is needed when you are perspiring like an overweight Turkish bath attendant. Luckily, a colleague was on hand with a deliciously cool lime cordial drink to quench my thirst and lower my body temperature.

The first one slipped down in a single gulp. It was a little sweet, but the tartness of the lime and the crushed ice made it perfectly refreshing. The second glass was equally welcome and dispatched with similar speed. We sat down for dinner and my host, the chair of the local chamber, offered me a glass of wine. Rather smugly I declined, explaining that I would stick to the thirst-quenching lime pop for now and have a glass of wine later. He looked at me slightly oddly, but I ignored him and continued trying to restore my equilibrium. Most importantly, I had to make sure that the jacket of my suit covered up the hideous perspiration stains now affecting nearly all of the pale blue shirt I was wearing. This required me to use my arms to keep my jacket pinned to my side. I could only eat and drink awkwardly using my wrists and hands. It was as if a very sweaty tyrannosaurus rex had come for dinner.

By the time I stood up to deliver my speech, I was feeling quite mellow, my biorhythms were back to almost normal and I was properly rehydrated. I took my speech from the inside pocket of my jacket, noting as I did that the sweat-map of the Peloponnese archipelago on my shirt had now faded to an acceptable degree. I opened my mouth to speak. Nothing happened. I tried again: the same. Somehow, between the appetiser and the entrée, I must have had root canal treatment and received a massive anaesthetic injection that had completely numbed my mouth, preventing the effective formulation of even the simplest words.

Caipirinha. I had been *caipirinhed.* Brazil's signature national cocktail had done me in. A lethal combination of distilled sugar cane – *cachaça* – and lime, sweetened and served with ice. It tastes like something you might give your kids at a children's birthday party but has the same effect as drinking fully leaded petroleum. Somehow, I must have stumbled through enough of my speech in an incoherent and garbled fashion, resorting to interpretative mime for the complicated bits, even if I have no recollection of what I said. This being generous, open-hearted Brazil – not stuffy judgemental London or New York – nobody seemed to mind, and I sat down to enthusiastic, if not rapturous, applause. My host leant over and cheekily offered me another *caipirinha*. Why not, I thought. What else can go wrong?

That sums up Brazil. One minute you find yourself in a viper's nest of criminality with a motley selection of undesirables. The next, you are among friends, enjoying the carefree, tolerant vibe of a society where nobody takes themselves too seriously – at least not at cocktail hour. It is the light and shade of Brazil. On the one hand, it makes the country so charming and appealing. On the other, it is what is so frustrating about a land with all the God-given plenitude any nation might want but with a darker side that stubbornly will not go away.

Rio epitomises that dichotomy. Think of the world's great harbour cities. Think of Cape Town, Sydney, Vancouver, Hong Kong. They are all magnificent. But Rio leaves them trailing in its wake. Viewed from the air, it is the most unusual landscape. The most notable feature being a series of hills shaped like exaggerated camels' humps dotted around the entrance to Baia de Guanabara at the point where Brazil's Serra do Mar mountains meet the Atlantic Ocean in a twisting amalgam of bays, islands and beaches. For geographical location alone, it is the most beautiful city in the world.

But look closer. The beaches are amazing, the bars

and restaurants are superb, the remnants of Rio's colonial architecture are magnificent and, as we have discovered, the local brew leaves you feeling decidedly tranquil – if not comatose. But the city cannot shake off its crime problem. Its notorious favelas – the unregulated, low-income neighbourhoods – dominate many of the slopes in the city. And in Rio, unlike many other great ocean-facing cities, the poor have the best views. Not all of the favelas are hot-beds of criminality; many are functioning mini-cities with their own community-based approach to civic life. But others are notorious no-go areas where drug gangs hold sway, and the homicide rate is among the highest in the world.

Every few years a new approach to tackling crime is introduced, and for a while some modest positive impact is made, not least during the 2016 Olympic Games, when we planned and coordinated security for thousands of sponsors, spectators and participants. Rio, in particular, is a hard place to keep people safe, not least because the relaxed beach culture masks quite how dangerous the city can be, and lulls new visitors into a false sense of security. But Brazil's persistent crime is multi-layered. Its roots stretch deep into the city's intestines; they are entwined far into the tangled knot of its endemic poverty, its vexed racial heritage and the internecine nature of organised crime. And it is inextricably linked to the potent power of the narcotics business. Multiple attempts have been made over the years to tackle the deep-seated social problems which give rise to criminality. Often the dysfunctionality of Brazil's national politics frustrates meaningful progress, as the country oscillates from military dictatorship to parliamentary democracy of various hues to right-wing populism. But what consistently frustrates progress is corruption.

Corruption is a scourge on any society. It is the enemy of progress and the root cause of so many ills that beset countries all over the world. Brazil is not the most corrupt country in the world. But it is one in which corruption has become deeply woven into public life and, for too long, has been tolerated as an inevitable way to get things done. Brazilians use the Portuguese word, *jeito* when talking about everyday bribery. It literally means a *way* but is commonly used to mean a fix or solution, often in response to a complex legal code that, some argue, encourages bribery. Compliance with the law is so complicated and cumbersome that you can almost justify paying bribes just to get something done. Applying for a building permit, for instance, is insanely and deliberately complicated, so that you can feel left with little choice other than to make some small facilitative arrangement on the side. I have had so many Brazilians explain this to me with a world-weary shrug of the shoulders that you can almost see their point. But what may seem harmless at this level spreads and infects every level of the economy.

You will repeatedly hear the claim that corruption is cultural in places like Brazil. It never is. The argument is nearly always used by people with a vested interest in the status quo. Being conditioned to small-scale, localised corruption sets the expectation that it is acceptable and part of the system. And then society adjusts around it. Senior politicians in Brazil have the right to appoint senior executives at the country's numerous state-backed industrial giants. These executives, in turn, it is claimed, solicit bribes, let contracts and then funnel that money back into the coffers of the political party that got them the job in the first place. It is a nepotistic, revolving form of patronage, and a corrosive blight on the health and efficiency of the economy and the political system. Corruption, more than anything else, is a form of social control and economic suppression. It is what keeps the poorest poor and the often undeserving, rich.

Brazilians have seen countless official campaigns launched to tackle corruption over the years. They have become inured to them and sceptical about their motivations and efficacy. But in 2014, even the most cynical were taken aback by the scale of the corruption probe that was launched into alleged wrongdoing at the national oil company, Petrobras. It became known as *Lava Jato* or Car Wash and it was the criminal investigation into corruption that spread to Brazil's other state-owned industries and deep into the economy. It upended a lot of corporate Brazil, sent top industrialists to prison, accused 80% of senators of fraud, toppled two presidents and sent one of the most powerful and popular former Presidents, Luiz Inácio da Silva – 'Lula' – to jail. What started out as a small-scale investigation into allegations of money-laundering through the activities of petrol stations (hence the name, Car Wash – or *Lava Jato* in Portuguese), erupted into one of the most far-reaching corruption purges anywhere in the world in recent years.

Lava Jato alone spawned a massive industry of lawyers and investigators poring over years-worth of documentation. I got to witness first-hand how complex these investigations can be and how far-reaching they can spread as my colleagues spent years working around the clock in shifts forensically interrogating the data, finding and interviewing witnesses and reconstructing the whole sorry tale, which stretched throughout Brazil and beyond.

What was unusual about *Lava Jato* was that it made life very uncomfortable for Brazil's protected, wealthy elite. Previous probes had generally stopped long before anybody with serious money or influence was likely to be affected. *Lava Jato* was an equal-opportunities investigation. Fuelled by a hitherto unseen public anger and driven forwards by a new generation of evangelical prosecutors, it gathered formidable momentum.

I remember meeting Marcelo Odebrecht, the scion of one of Brazil's most notable industrial families, well before the investigation was launched. At the time, there was no hint of what was to come. Marcelo was the epitome of urbane charm. US-educated, he was the poster-boy of the new Brazil. I only met him briefly, but he seemed like a breath of fresh air after the many Brazilian business grandees that I had met previously, who, for all their smooth patter and oleaginous ways, were so obviously up to their necks in cronyism and graft. In normal times, Marcelo would expect to be well above the high-tide mark of even the most rigorous of corruption probes. But these were not normal times, and he went to jail.

People like Marcelo rarely regard themselves as criminal. They either see themselves as being so important in what they do that somehow the normal rules do not apply to them or they have become so blinkered and cosseted that they cannot see their own actions with any form of honest objectivity. It is not just the rich and famous that suffer from this kind of delusion. Many people shift through a process of gradation from innocent to guilty. At some stage, they transgress. It might be some minor infringement that over time they justify in their mind and rationalise to the point that they genuinely do not think they have done anything wrong. Or they just assume that common practice means acceptable practice. They become conditioned to wrongdoing to such an extent that they no longer distinguish right from wrong.

Good has turned to bad, not through a single dramatic act or through some preordained genetic delinquency but incrementally, over time and without a moral Rubicon being crossed. And the powerful live very often in echo chambers where nobody questions their actions, and nobody confronts them with the bald truth. Most often, this is how corruption and malfeasance become engrained in big business. Not by secret criminal conspiracy or by widespread conscious ethical failure but by stealth. Mostly, members of the top economic class do not self-identify as criminals. They are careful to distance themselves from the egregious extremes of fraudulent behaviour. But they help create and perpetuate a way of doing business that is rotten.

It could be that the world actually does cleave into good and evil, and that all attempts to look for shade are just a way to excuse the behaviour of people who have mislaid their moral compass and are wandering lost in a fog of moral turpitude. But I hope I can still distinguish between someone who is trying to navigate a tricky course as honestly as they can in countries not blessed with long traditions of strong institutional behaviour and the out-and-out fraudster.

When I started out in the risk business, corruption was not an easy subject to discuss publicly. In many countries, it was still an acceptable means of doing business and in some cases even a tax-deductible expense. That has changed. It is still a massive problem, but now major international corporations fall over themselves to parade their anti-corruption and ethical credentials. Big business talks about establishing what they call *tone from the top*. Making sure that the CEO and other senior executives consistently and routinely espouse the view that they do not pay bribes. The message has to be clear: that sort of thing is not how business is done around here, so do not even bother to ask.

Tone from the top is great – up to a point. But I have seen the messy consequences on many occasions where fine words at Davos are not matched on the ground in some faraway subsidiary where the business is locked into a complex series of joint-venture vehicles with dodgy partners in a country with a poor track-record in corporate integrity. I have sat with prominent Brazilian industrialists who have boasted of their role as the bribe-paying junior partner in international consortia. What matters here is less the tone from the top and more the *tone from the middle* – what the people actually charged with running the business do on the ground. Needless to say, there is often a massive disconnect between the fine-sounding sentiments of the top brass and those toiling away in the engine room.

Corruption is like drug-taking – doping – in sport. Not so long ago, it was, in some sports, an open secret, a commonplace technique to enhance athletic performance. Gradually public opinion shifted from acceptance to tolerance to disquiet to intolerance and on to outrage as the drugs got stronger and the violations more egregious. As the practice becomes increasingly unacceptable, it goes further underground and gets more hidden. At the same time, unscrupulous doctors devise new ways of obtaining the same pharmaceutical boost as banned substances previously provided but using technical loopholes in the rules to 'prescribe' medically approved treatments. Substitute unscrupulous doctors for dodgy lawyers and the near-identical process has been at work in the corporate world to make bribery both harder to detect and not technically illegal, or at least so complicated no average jury has a clue what has happened.

It is not just corruption that holds Brazil back and it is not just Brazil that is held back by corruption. But at some stage during every dinner with Brazilian friends, the conversation will turn to what it is that prevents Brazil from progressing apace. Metaphors abound. When will the sleeping giant awake? When will we stop driving with the handbrake on? There is something about the scale and mass of Brazil that makes it feel like a country that is hard to change and reform. It is as big as the continental USA and the EU would fit within Brazil's boundaries. Brazil's 200 million people represent a diverse cross-section of ethnicities with massive socio-economic disparity. But the ruling elite, on the other hand, is like a village; they all seem to know each other.

Despite the very obvious inequities in how the country's natural bounty is shared, it has a clear sense of itself as a nation. It has never really had any material border disputes and tolerates its near neighbours, even if many of the upper class more naturally gravitate to the US or Europe than they do to the rest of Latin America. It has been a nation state longer than Italy or Germany. Like the United States, it has a sense of its own exceptionalism, and again, like America, ostentatious sexual freedom runs alongside moral rectitude. It is a more socially conservative country than a stroll along the beach in Rio might suggest.

Brazilians have a number of national preoccupations, one of which is complaining about their politicians. Every meal I have had with friends in Brazil has consisted of voluble complaints about their national leaders. It is a country that wants – but rarely has – national political icons that they can rally around. This may be why so many Brazilians from all backgrounds decided to take a punt on the right-wing populist Jair Bolsonaro to become president. He co-opted the anti-corruption agenda and then polarised the nation. But politics is by no means the most important thing on Brazilians' minds. At some stage during dinner, the genius that was Ayrton Senna, the brilliant Brazilian Formula One racing driver who died in a crash at the San Marino Grand Prix in 1994, will be acknowledged. This is a rite of passage that must be observed. Indeed, if you arrive by air into São Paulo, Brazil's main business centre, your taxi driver will most probably take Rua Ayrton Senna on the journey into town. At which point you will realise that the great racing driver is not just a national icon, but a motoring role model. Nearly all Brazilian motorists will, at some stage, take the opportunity to emulate the speed and risk-taking pathology of the great man.

Of course, Brazilians are also obsessed by football. It does not matter if you are young or old, rich or poor, black or white, from the north or the south, from the coast or the Amazon, from some grand luxury mansion or the worst of the favelas. This vast, contradictory country just loves soccer. They call it *O jogo bonito*, the beautiful game. The sport was introduced into Brazil in 1894 by the son of a Scottish railway engineer and to say that Brazilians have adopted the game and made it their own is an understatement. Soccer has given this country a sense of nationhood like nothing else and, in genius players like Pele, it has provided proxy-leaders, heroes and role models. Its World Cup record has given the country the sweet taste of great triumph and the bitter pill of humiliation. When Brazil hosted the World Cup in 2014 and lost 7-1 to Germany in the semi-final, it was a national disaster on a scale that is hard to fathom. Soccer is not just the national sport; it is a large part of the national identity. It makes everything just seem better.

Perhaps that is where I went wrong with *O Coronel*. Rather than sitting there, frozen with apprehension and discomfort,

I should have switched the conversation to soccer. He would have relaxed, even smiled maybe. His henchmen would have sat down and opened some beers – or no doubt mixed up a *caipirinha* or two – before explaining that they were not in fact a squad of ruthless black ops mercenaries operating far beyond the reach of the law, but a team of hard-working forensic accountants just looking to do an honest day's work.

8

Functional dysfunctionality

PRIME MINISTER'S QUESTION TIME in the Indian parliament in Delhi is a raucous occasion. Based in the grand Sansad Bhavan – originally built to house the Imperial Legislative Council – this is the epicentre of the world's largest democracy. It is worth a visit. You can witness just what noisy and rumbustious theatre democracy can be. Members of Parliament get very animated and histrionic, often getting up from their seat to run to the centre of the semi-circular debating chamber to hotly remonstrate with their opposite numbers. On the day I attended, parliament was debating a proposed ban on plastic shopping bags. A worthy cause, but the level of passion and histrionics on display was more indicative of an imminent nuclear attack or extraterrestrial visitation than a sensible measure to curb retail pollution.

A number of members of parliament wear the particular local dress from the specific part of India that they represent, a visual reminder of the vastness and diversity of this country.

Likewise, the banks of translators, covering the twenty-two official languages recognised by the parliament, give you a further sense of the complexity of making the democratic process work on such a grand scale. If the members of parliament are allowed a lot of latitude in the way they behave, visitors by contrast are expected to adhere to strict rules of protocol and decorum. I was admonished and threatened with ejection by the ushers in the visitors' gallery on no fewer than five occasions for the following offences: whispering to my neighbour; crossing my legs; fanning myself with my visitor pass; whispering again and pointing at Sonia Gandhi – a parliamentarian and the late prime minister's widow.

The parliament is part of a grand collection of government buildings in New Delhi that were designed in the twentieth century by a team led by the British architect, Edwin Lutyens. They constitute one of the boldest projections of political authority in any capital city. Sitting atop a low hill, they comprise the Indian parliament, the presidential residence and a selection of administrative buildings. They are surrounded by a vast acreage of green space in the heart of the city. A short distance down the hill from the official home of the President of India, through public-access parkland, sits the majestic India Gate, a war memorial on an epic scale. When they were built, nearly a hundred years ago, these buildings were a clear demonstration of British imperial self-confidence. Houses, railways and canals were moved to make way for their construction – nothing, it seemed, was too much for this celebration of the durability of British colonial rule. As it turned out they were anything but. Rather than being an icon of empire, Lutyens' Delhi became a testament to the perils of hubris.

India Gate was completed in 1931, around the same time

as the rest of the buildings. Within sixteen years, the British empire in India was over. The colonial government had hastily partitioned the country into India and Pakistan, packed its bags, handed the keys over to the new owners and set sail for Blighty. After World War Two, the British government, near bankrupt and exhausted by six years of war, had other more pressing domestic priorities than prolonging Britain's presence on the subcontinent. India had gone from being the jewel in the crown to a millstone around a changing nation's neck.

Rather than being a celebration of the benign might of Britain, these buildings serve as a pertinent reminder that just when you think you are on top of your game, fortunes can and often do turn on a sixpence. It happens to empires, countries, their leaders, film stars, sports stars and celebrity entrepreneurs. It is not a certainty – every generation has the occasional figure whose success and reputation are enduring – but, in my experience, success and failure are close bedfellows. After several decades of running a business all around the world, this is either the only thing I have learned or the one universal truth that informs everything else I know. Just when you are sure that you are on top of your game, that you have now got the hang of whatever it is you do, that you have crawled to the top of your particular hill, then almost certainly something is about to go wrong.

That creeping sense of self-satisfaction should be what rings alarm bells in our head. A great clanging Big Ben of a warning, alerting us to imminent peril. But most often the bells remain un-rung. It is a lesson that we, champion recidivists, are destined to repeat time and time again, failing to learn from experience. I do not understand the scientific, sociological or neurological rationale for why this happens. I just know that it is true.

To be fair, these buildings nowadays do not feel like a redundant embarrassing relic from a bygone era. Somehow, they work as a part of the mosaic heritage that makes up modern India. And India Gate stands – like war memorials should – not as an affirmation of the cause for which the wars were fought but as a testament to those who died fighting them.

This is a country that will assault your senses. To get a sense of just how assaulted you will be, leave the grandeur of New Delhi and head to its more typically Indian counterpart, Old Delhi. By bicycle. As a primer on the multiple contradictions that comprise modern India, this jolting combination of order and chaos will set you up for what will follow. Old Delhi is a section of the capital loosely grouped around the Red Fort, the former home of the Mughal emperors and where, on 15 August 1947, India's first prime minister, Jawaharlal Nehru, raised the Indian national flag to mark the country's independence. This part of the city has miraculously been left alone by the developers. It offers the opportunity to observe a slice of Delhi not seen from the terrace of Delhi's many international hotels. Given Delhi's appalling traffic and even worse pollution, a bicycle may seem an odd and hazardous choice of transportation. It is certainly not the healthy or low-risk option, but it is a practical means of covering a lot of ground and an experience you will not readily forget.

Old Delhi was constructed in the seventeenth century along with the Red Fort, and other than the introduction of electricity – in great swags of cabling snaking above and around your head – not much seems to have changed. It is a whirl of activity. Food is being prepared that requires the chasing, catching and dispatching of chickens. Everything you could imagine is being sold, from car parts to bras to trotters to exotic spices that will make your eyes sting. As in so many places in India, you will encounter children somehow contriving to play a makeshift game of cricket in among the crowded lanes. Everybody seems to be incredibly busy, even if it is not entirely clear what they are up to.

In and among these streets you get a sense of the infinite types of endeavour that constitute this great, sprawling, hard to regulate, harder to measure economy. And if navigating tiny, twisting alleyways on a bicycle is not hard enough, great care needs to be taken to avoid the ubiquitous cows that roam the back streets. Serene and adulated, they are given priority and protection by their sanctity. They wander at will, as if they are well aware of their special status. It is a bicycle assault-course of the most unusual kind through a part of the city whose functional dysfunctionality is – in microcosm – the epitome of the country as a whole. You get a first-hand view of how poor much of India still is, how adaptable and resourceful it can be, how young its people are, the sense of industriousness and purpose with which people go about their business and the huge deficit India still faces in much of its basic infrastructure. No doubt, Old Delhi is an affront to city planners with a mandate to modernise India but, for now, they have not yet got their hands on it.

India defies being learnt. It has to be experienced. That may sound like a truism for any country and of course each nation has its own personality quirks that only reveal themselves over time, as you dig deeper into the fabric of the place and understand what makes it tick. Yet there is something in the scale and lack of anything approaching homogeneity that makes India more of a challenge than most places. Nevertheless, people arrive with their stereotypical assumptions about India, not least the British. There is something about being the former colonial power that gives some people a false sense of what they think Indians want to hear. In my experience, they are tired of being told that we speak the same language, enjoy our version of their food and that we both play cricket. That is not to say there are not deep bonds of family and affection between the two nations, but it is easy to get bogged down in Britain's own cultural heritage and miss the fact that India does not want to be defined by what the British once tried to create here. Over time, I think India slowly reveals itself, but it is hard to try to force the pace, even though many people attempting to do business in India cannot afford to spend a lifetime allowing the mystique of the land to slowly worm its way into their subconscious.

Of course, you can sit down and plough your way through the swathes of material that have been written about India. And there is no shortage of easily accessible Indian journalism. The number of newspapers, magazines, periodicals, blogs and news outlets is mind-boggling. I have been interviewed by many different journalists in India, ranging from the seriously well-informed to the ones whom you sense may have just come to your office to enjoy the air-conditioning. What they all have in common is a persistence to keep asking you questions to which either you do not know the answer or are reluctant to say if you do. And given the Indian facility with English idiom, there are always seemingly endless ways to ask the same thing.

On one occasion, I was interviewed by a senior reporter from one of India's top television stations and for some reason the interview was to take place in my hotel. Due to a mix-up with the hotel's meeting rooms, it was necessary at the last minute to film the interview in my bedroom. The crew arrived and set up the cameras and the lights and arranged the chairs in a corner of the room so that my pyjamas, toothbrush and other personal effects were not in shot.

My interviewer arrived with unusual punctuality. She was in her mid to late sixties and we were set to discuss the global political outlook for the year ahead. She was dressed immaculately in a sari and had the kind of natural authority, poise and erudition that immediately made me even more gauche and clumsy than usual. She also had an encyclopaedic knowledge of world affairs and a serious-minded, intense demeanour to match. To try to lighten the mood for what I realised was going to be an exhausting tour of the world's geopolitical complexities, I made some ill-advised and slightly smutty quips about how often either of us found ourselves in a bedroom with a film crew. It was intended as a light-hearted, mildly racy comment to break the ice and establish an informal mood, more conducive to my remembering arcane details about the global economy.

But I knew as soon as the words left my mouth that this was a dumb thing to say. She looked at me over the top of her spectacles: 'I am sorry', she said inquisitorially, 'what do you mean? Please explain.' I realised to my horror that the cameras had already started rolling and the interview was underway. I managed to throw up a barrage of bluster and back-tracking sufficient to avoid too much immediate embarrassment.

But my inquisitor was not going to let me off so easily for this obvious breach of propriety and decorum. This was clearly the first time anybody had even jokingly connected her to a porn film. It was evidently a violation of her stern code of moral rectitude, so the gloves were off. She immediately asked me about the likelihood of armed conflict between India and Pakistan – a nightmare question for any executive wanting to do business in both countries to answer on the public record. I tried my best to slip sideways into simmering tensions in the Middle East. When she ignored that, I fell back on an old trick that normally works in India. I suggested that China's stellar economic growth may be coming to an end and that India may be catching up. This is nearly always an easy red herring for Indian journalists, who ordinarily like nothing more than the idea that their great rival, China, is losing some of its economic lustre. She did not buy it and instead kept me pinned to the ropes. I ducked and weaved, absorbed some substantial body blows and kept my gloves up, but eventually sank to my knees.

On another occasion, I managed to double-book myself. I had arranged to have lunch with the political editor of India's top newspaper on the terrace of one of Delhi's smartest hotels, The Imperial. At the same time, I was also meant to be the *talking head* on a TV current affairs programme broadcast from Mumbai. I was to be beamed via satellite link to Mumbai from a remote studio set up in one of the upstairs rooms in the Imperial. Rather than come clean and drop one of the scheduled commitments, I decided to wing it. I had the first course of the lunch on the terrace, discussing the current state of Indian politics. Prime Minister Modi had made a promising start but had yet to really translate bold intentions into implementable policies. Foreign investors were still waiting to see tangible progress in the reform of India's tangled web of a tax code. At this point, my PR adviser, and accomplice in this ludicrous subterfuge, Rahmat, arrived at the table to say that there was a dire emergency in the Middle East (entirely plausible), and I was wanted on the telephone immediately. I apologised to my guest, walked sedately out of view and then Rahmat and I sprinted through the hotel, ran up the stairs, slipping and sliding along a long corridor with a highly polished tiled floor and burst into the makeshift TV studio. I breathlessly explained again how the slowing of the Chinese economy was going to put pressure on global commodity prices. When they went to an ad break in Mumbai, we rushed downstairs again just in time for the main course. We pulled off this ludicrous charade one more time before, thankfully, we finished lunch, the bemused correspondent left, and the TV show came to an end. The indefatigable Rahmat and I collapsed into the bar and ordered a drink.

If dealing with India's journalists can be tricky then so can some Indian clients. Nearly every conversation starts with a lecture by them on how little they can afford to pay for the advice they say they want. There is nothing unique about India in this. I have had lots of super-rich clients claim impecuniosity. Dealing with this requires a thick skin and the ability to nod sympathetically, agree to re-look at a revised scope and at how the overall pricing model might be restructured, and then give absolutely no ground. Often, listening to the poverty speech is at odds with the contradictory visual clues suggested by opulently decorated palatial offices filled with expensive art. Others seem to deliberately occupy the most low-rent offices imaginable so that they can play the impecunious card with greater authenticity.

Indian clients have this dance down to a tee. One client in Mumbai was once giving me the usual routine about the need for us to work at an enormous discount. We were sitting in his mould-damp, putrid office, straining to hear what he was saying above the noise of the ancient, wheezing, utterly ineffective air-conditioning unit hanging precariously from the only window in the room. A machine so useless, I am sure it was making the room even hotter, not cooler. As if on cue, an enormous cockroach ran out from under a cupboard and scuttled around on the floor between us. I have a feeling it was either radio-controlled, operated by a secret button under his desk or else it was real and very well-trained. Either way, the creature's timing could not have been better and the general grime – complete absence of anything that could vaguely be described as art – and the presence of vermin added some authenticity to his claims of impoverishment.

Our own office in Delhi in the early days had a resident rat. He lived in the bathroom – the office also served as an apartment – apparently on an exclusive diet of toothpaste. Eventually he was trapped, with due concern for Hindu sensitivities about not causing harm to living creatures, and re-housed in the local park. Within hours, he was back. Turned out he was a homing-rat, or else, he just loved the minty-freshness of the toothpaste. But the decrepitude in which corporate India is housed is misleading. Many Indian companies out-compete the best in the world. Many of them started as family businesses and, despite the fact they have morphed into enormous, worldwide conglomerates, they retain many of those core entrepreneurial, boot-strap qualities. They are adaptable; decision-making is not hampered by excessive governance and they are very often risking their own capital, not that of remote, faceless shareholders. But the dynastic nature of big Indian business can be labyrinthine in its complexity.

Over the years many foreign clients have chosen to hitch their wagons to India's big family concerns as an effective way of navigating a market that can otherwise be so opaque. This is usually quite a smart idea but not risk-free. For what these families do spectacularly well is fall out among themselves and with each other. And when they do, the consequences can be explosive. I have spent hours with foreign executives who have limped bewildered into our office having found themselves caught up in a whirlwind of familial vindictiveness, revenge and wickedness that makes the Borgias look like the Waltons.

This is the type of risk that snags investors the most in India. Rarely is India physically dangerous for foreign visitors, outside of Kashmir and other restless corners of the country. The Mumbai attacks of 2008 were a murderous exception. Ten members of Lashkar-e-Taiba, a Pakistan-based group, launched a sea-borne assault on various luxury hotels and other buildings along Mumbai's seafront. The attack lasted four days and resulted in the deaths of 174 people. The ten terrorists were well-trained, drilled and equipped with explosives and heavy weaponry. One of them, Ajmal Kasab was captured alive by the Indian authorities; the rest were killed. The attacks were carefully targeted both to inflict high numbers of casualties and to attract maximum international attention. The two hotels that were attacked are among India's most prestigious, and on the day of the attacks, many senior Indian and international politicians and businesspeople were resident in them. By day two, the attackers were holed up in the hotels and the perimeter was surrounded by troops from India's National Security Guard.

These are India's elite troops, nicknamed the Black Cats. They were formed after the assassination of Prime Minister Indira Gandhi and trained for occasions like this. We had numerous clients in the targeted hotels and were able to communicate with them from the edge of the security cordon by mobile phone. Unusually, the mobile network was still up and running in the first few hours of what had now effectively become a siege situation as the Black Cats prepared to enter the buildings. We advised them what to do: stay away from the windows at all costs, lie in the bath, keep their phones on and charging for as long as possible but not to use them. We passed messages to their loved ones to discourage them from calling and texting. We were also able to relay their coordinates to the authorities as they built up a picture of where the hostages were in the building. Critically, we also helped them understand what to expect when the Black Cats entered their room and how to know that it was them and not the terrorists. It would not be the discreet knock of expensive room service.

It was a long night and morning until the operation was complete. The Black Cats rescued 550 people from the hotels and averted even greater bloodshed. Our clients emerged shocked and, in some cases, traumatised by their experience. They had not gone on business to a war zone. This was downtown Mumbai, one of the most vibrant business centres in the world, and they had no reason to expect something like this was going to happen. That it rarely does is little comfort for those people unfortunate enough to be caught up in the middle of the attacks.

Doing business in India is not just about getting used to the complexities and surprises that such a weirdly wonderful country serves up with such regularity. It is about suspending expectations. In nearly all the countries I have got to know over the years, there is some attempt at crafting a singular national story about where the country is heading. Some countries do it better than others. China, the emergent great power, taking its rightful place close to the apex of global power, does it in a more sustained and homogenous fashion than most. Others, such as post-war Japan and West Germany, were able to articulate their future in terms of escaping the cataclysm that had engulfed them – only for that focus to blur when prosperity blunts the imperative and memories fade.

Presidents Trump, Putin and Xi defined themselves as the restorers of lost greatness even if they would not acknowledge their common goal and similar motivation. People respond to and follow politicians who provide them with a compelling narrative about their shared moment in their nation's history. The reality of any leadership role is that it is around 80% heroic improvisation, responding to random events and sudden reversals of fortune. But that is a hard sell. Politicians instead seek office offering a fresh start and a manifesto of planned change. We all need to write our own script.

India is no exception. Under Prime Minister Modi, India has been given a new national story. A nation whose time has come, even if it comes with a much harder edge of Hindu nationalism. A vision of a prosperous, technocratic global power that has escaped its colonial legacy, will stand shoulder to shoulder with China and is treated respectfully by the United States. Where the vast informal economy will be corralled. Where India's inefficient and decrepit national infrastructure will be revitalised. Where the creative genius that spawned Bollywood will achieve international recognition. Where opportunity and education will break the vice-like poverty trap. And where the country's enormous technological expertise will be harnessed to make India an advanced manufacturing economy that will entice the vast and highly successful Indian diaspora home again.

Some version of this vision will be realised, I am sure. No doubt it will be repackaged many times over and the focus will shift from a busy domestic agenda to foreign affairs. That is the usual pattern. Politicians of all stripes often start by winning an election with the promise of material improvement in people's lives. When that proves tricky to implement and popularity has waned, they switch to seeking compensatory prestige on the international stage. The hope for India is that, as reform and modernisation falters, it does not get burnt by the easy-to-fan flames of sectarian conflict or side-tracked by vainglorious projects, like the British did in the final days of imperial rule.

India has made extraordinary progress in the past twenty years, giving millions of Indians the opportunity to realise their natural gifts and potential. But contradictions remain. This is a country that has spawned some world-class global companies but where some 85% of Indians are self-employed in micro enterprises. Where a new billionaire class lives in close proximity to millions still living in heart-stopping poverty. Where some women rise to the top in politics and business, but many others are still subject to discrimination and abuse. A country where national politicians, housed in colonial magnificence, are still wrestling for authority with all-powerful local politicians and landowners. Where the enormous cultural, religious, linguistic and ethnic diversity of India, which is so captivating as you travel around the country, frustrates efforts to forge a unifying national consensus. And where the government of a nation with an advanced space programme still fails to provide the basic infrastructure to stop people shitting in the street.

And therein is what makes India distinctive: everything is on display. Little, it seems, is hidden from public view. The dynamism, the creativity, the mysticism, and the majesty of Lutyens' architectural genius are all there to be seen from the saddle of your bicycle. And so is the poverty, the cruelty and the squalor. All of it is India and you have no choice but to take it as it comes.

9

Big, brash and brilliant

I AM A FULLY ACCREDITED member of the Lagos fan club. We are a select band, dedicated in our affection and often swimming against the tide of popular opinion. Many business travellers and local residents find Nigeria's largest city an abhorrent assault on their senses. But as fans we appreciate the vibrancy, optimism and dynamism of this sprawling mega-city. It has an almost unique energy. Much of it channelled to nefarious ends, for sure, but the place is extraordinarily energetic, nevertheless.

Nigerian street markets, for instance, have got to be the purest form of capitalism. They sell a bewildering array of goods and services in what seems like a chaotic explosion of intense entrepreneurial frenzy. There are very few barriers to entry, and you have multiple people selling the same thing, ensuring that prices are determined by something close to perfect competition, not distorted by monopolies and cartels. Ingenuity and a casual disregard for intellectual property mean that what is on offer is determined directly by consumer demand, not by the market-warping power of big brands. Should your expensive smartphone suspiciously stop working around the time a new model is introduced to great fanfare, you have no need to expensively upgrade. A dexterous-fingered Nigerian teenager is on-hand to dismantle your existing phone and fix it, thereby enabling you to neatly dodge the inbuilt obsolescence that encourages frivolous, wasteful materialism and swells the profits of big tech.

Much of Lagos is controlled by so-called Area Boys. These are gangs of adolescents who openly and often quite cheerfully extort regular small payments from stallholders and vendors. They are ubiquitous, patrolling the markets, stores and traffic jams of the country's major urban centres. Their ranks are swelled by the lack of formal education and employment prospects among Nigeria's urban poor. You see them knocking on the windows of buses, sometimes masquerading as police officers in poorly fitting improvised uniforms. Occasionally, they will provide some kind of service in exchange for a few *naira* – a perfunctory wash of your windscreen perhaps – but mostly it is just a demand for money with nothing in return other than the relief of being temporarily left alone by the boys and their Fagin-like bosses.

Life as a street-trader is not for the faint-hearted. Any slip in performance and someone will take your place; failure to pay your dues and the joviality of the Area Boys will be replaced by the menace of impending violence. You also need vast reserves of optimism. I was once queuing to enter the departure terminal at Lagos airport when I was approached to see if I was interested in purchasing an iron and ironing board. The salesman would have noted that I was dressed in a suit and he would probably have spotted that I was getting highly stressed and irascible as I was already very late for my flight and the check-in line snaked out of the terminal building. Perhaps he thought, 'I know what this chap needs for the flight home. He needs an ironing board.'

Having been well brought-up by my parents, I politely but firmly mouthed, 'No thank you, not today,' in the same way my mother did to gypsies who came door to door selling tea towels and clothes pegs. He seemed surprised and then affronted, baffled as to why an iron and ironing board, complete with a spare cover, was not the immediate solution to my obvious distress. Perhaps he thought I might want to while away the long hours on the flight back to Europe by setting up the ironing board in the aisle of the passenger cabin and pressing a few shirts. Having got my attention, he quickly dropped the laundry-related offer and proposed other services that he could render. Services of a more carnal and narcotic nature. There must have been something about the harassed executive vibe I was conveying that indicated that he might have more luck with this part of the service range. Again, I tried to decline the offer as politely as possible but not before my Nigerian companion had issued some curt rebuke to him to push off. He picked up his ironing boards, put them across his shoulder and moved on to the next person in the queue. But before he did, he fixed me with a haughty and imperious look to make it clear that it was I, not he, who had just missed out on the commercial transaction of the decade and that the loss was all mine.

This young man no doubt does this all day long, every day, all year round. This is not surprising in a city of somewhere in the region of 20 million people, with a massive informal economy and an impoverished underclass. Indeed, there are millions of people like this street-seller all around the world.

This unremitting cycle of toil is what passes for normal life for more people than most of us can possibly imagine. Nigeria is no exception. But there is something special about the Nigerians when it comes to the manner with which they go about their business. They do so with extraordinary ingenuity, confidence and whatever the African version of chutzpah is called in Hausa, Yoruba or Igbo. The day before my near purchase of the ironing board, the Lagos municipal authorities (yes, such a body exists despite the evident anarchy) had introduced yet another attempt to make it compulsory for motorcyclists to wear crash helmets in the city. I saw several riders pass police roadblocks with saucepans on their heads and one enterprising woman astride her moped wearing a hollowed-out watermelon.

Poverty, poor education and a lack of anything approaching regular employment opportunities leave my ironing-board salesman and legions of other hard-grafting traders with little option other than to sell whatever they can on the streets. But he goes about his business with a purposefulness and intent that can make you feel pampered and ponderous, fey and feckless by comparison. This might be the very bottom broken rung of capitalism's rusted ladder, but he conducts himself with the confident air of an aspiring entrepreneur not with the subdued wretchedness of the terminally downtrodden. There is more hustle in Nigeria than anywhere else I know. Not surprisingly, American business schools are now falling over each other to study how Lagos' commercial ecosystems function. This is private enterprise in its rawest most visceral form. It is the premier-grade sashimi of economics, still twitching with freshness.

We need to bottle this. We need to find a way to extract whatever genetic code is imprinted onto this man's DNA and add it like fluoride to the drinking water. Politicians pontificating about poor productivity, millennials whining about work-life balance, able-bodied retirees permanently glued to day-time television quiz shows; what they all need is a good squirt of whatever it is that gets this bloke up and going in the morning. It isn't just escaping abject poverty that is the incentive – although that is obviously a big part of it – it is something distinctly Nigerian that provides the rocket fuel to strive. Take a good look at Nigeria and you might get a glimpse of the future.

Nigeria throbs. It is livid with potential. It is a country of over 200 million people, although nobody knows quite how many for sure. It will, according to the UN, overtake the US by 2047 to become the third most populous country in the world. This assumes that Nigerians maintain their current enthusiasm for reproduction, which is likely, given the hours they seem to put in on the training field. For now, the population continues to grow at double the world average and 44% of Nigerians are under 15. The median age is 18, compared to 48 in Japan. In a few years' time, when the rest of us are old and senile, bright young Nigerians will be running the world – or at least owning our care homes.

It has a diaspora that blows other diasporas out of the water. They are successful wherever they go and remit more cash back home than Nigeria receives in international aid. Global companies and public bodies are awash with brilliant Nigerians. Nollywood is one of the world's most prolific film industries, indicative of the creative, industrious dynamo that is so distinctly Nigerian. This is also a nation of snappy dressers. I once gave my driver in Lagos a pair of my shoes. They had never really fitted me properly and he seemed to be the right size. He felt obliged to appear grateful but you could tell that he knew they were way too dull and conventional for his high sartorial standards. And the country has one quality above all else that gives it the edge: it doesn't feel sorry for itself. It has that key FYA ingredient. FYA is an important political science concept but oddly one that is not taught at graduate school. It denotes those countries whose innate positivity overcomes all sorts of socio-economic challenges. It stands for Fuck You Attitude.

This place could really rock. It has already overtaken South Africa as Africa's biggest economy. Lagos alone is Africa's fifth biggest economy and more than 50% of Nigeria's population now lives in the cities – a key ingredient in fuelling GDP growth. Economists and investors salivate at what might be the continent's first economic superpower. But all these folks share one thing in common: they all see Nigeria through the distorting mesh of a spreadsheet. If data and statistics alone were a guarantee of success then I would be advising you to throw this book away immediately, sell your home, auction as many vital organs as you can spare, mortgage your children's future and stick it all on the roulette wheel of Nigeria's incipient record-busting boom.

But swotty, pointy-headed investors, with their logical, linear thought processes, often fail to take into account that for all its God-given plenitude, this is a country that is also riven with human fault-lines. It is a country that fought one of the most vicious civil wars in modern times, leaving a schism that still renders the political system almost inoperable. It has robbed itself of its own oil wealth on a jaw-dropping scale since the 1970s (values vary, but $400 billion is a reasonable estimate). Of the $100 million in daily oil sales, about 80% of the proceeds end up in the hands of 1% of the population. This is gush-up not trickle-down economics.

For too many people with access to power, it has been easier to get rich by exploiting the intricate web of nepotism and cronyism that surrounds Nigeria's oil industry than it has been to pursue any other form of regularised commercial activity. South Korea and Taiwan were approximately in the same economic boat as Nigeria in the early 1960s. But they were mostly devoid of natural resources and had to rely instead on the ingenuity of their human capital. Both countries have now streaked ahead. Nigerians are more than a match for anyone when it comes to raw potential, but they have been diverted by the addictive, destructive, corrupting bonanza of bountiful oil.

The population is split roughly 50:50 between Muslims and Christians who rub along well enough most of the time. But woven into this religious mix are 250 distinct ethnic groups speaking 500 languages and who often rub each other up the wrong way. Tens of millions of Nigerians live on less than $2 per day and the country lags behind places like Pakistan in poverty reduction. Notoriously, it has its own particularly odious and nihilistic terrorist outfit, Boko Haram. Communal violence, fuelled by endemic poverty, is a sad feature of daily life for too many Nigerians and briefly came to international attention during the Lagos riots against allegations of police brutality in 2020. Sometimes, the country can fix its own problems in the most astonishing ways; in 2014, Nigeria managed to contain the Ebola virus when the massed ranks of its armchair critics were predicting a devastating pandemic. But the sepsis of venality and corruption has infected nearly every aspect of public life.

A retired diplomat friend served as ambassador consecutively in the United Arab Emirates, Indonesia and finally Nigeria in the 1990s. He describes how, after a few years in the Gulf, he felt he understood how corruption worked. It was endemic to the ruling elite but there were unspoken limits to individual venality which enabled the country to function with superficial legitimacy. In Indonesia, he realised that graft spread way beyond the power brokers in Jakarta and was deeply rooted and localised right across a dispersed and fragmented nation. When he arrived in Abuja, he realised that to date he had only been watching amateurs at work. These people were looting professionally and on an industrial scale. But of the three countries, Nigeria was – by a long chalk – his favourite country.

Corruption takes many forms. On landing in Lagos you need to produce a certificate showing that you have had the appropriate inoculations against yellow fever in order to pass through immigration. On one occasion, I was in a hurry, so I made it to immigration before any of my fellow passengers. The border official squinted at my yellow fever certificate and declared it invalid (it was not). I had a choice, he explained. I could pay him a cash *fine* of $200 or have a yellow fever injection there and then. I looked over at the dubious-looking nurse who was ready to inject me using a hypodermic needle of doubtful hygiene. I protested the validity of my certificate until more passengers started to arrive. When the official was momentarily distracted by the prospect of new targets, I ran off, and hid behind a taxi outside when he came looking for me.

Nigeria is the big brash epitome of why it is so tricky to know anything about the future with even a modicum of certainty. It also gives us an insight into how difficult it is to understand the intermittent relationship between what is risky and what is not. Optimists look at the place, examine what is going on and see wealth and prosperity within almost immediate reach. Pessimists examine the same facts and figures and see only disaster and mayhem. Meanwhile, well-meaning realists like me are torn between our head and our heart. We badly want the place to break out of the cycle of misgovernance but realistically we doubt it will do so any time soon.

It is not just Nigeria. The world used to obsess about the so-called BRICS countries, a term invented by Goldman Sachs in 2001. The idea was that Brazil, Russia, India, China and (later) South Africa were the up-and-coming countries as their growth rates accelerated in a globalised economy. The notion turned out to be generally right, even if in practice it was specifically wrong. China found the back of the net in the first few minutes and never really looked back. India started well but then trailed off in the second half. Brazil ran onto the pitch waving to their ecstatic fans but then failed to put any kind of game plan into action. Russia briefly talked a good muscular game but never really got started. And South Africa, somewhat lucky to be on the team sheet in the first place, is now back on the bench.

Later, there was much hype over the so-called MINT countries. Nigeria was joined by Mexico, Indonesia and Turkey. The same dynamic applies. It turns out that crafting neat acronyms is the easy bit and the MINTs concept was soon holed below the waterline. Of course, you can open the à la carte menu of available data, and build arguments to explain why each of these countries is poised for greatness. Equally, you can select from the same menu and find umpteen reasons why their coming economic renaissance will be kicked down the street. Nobody really knows what is going to happen and herein lies the opportunity. If you are at a loose end, try selecting a random group of countries. The only criterion for selection is that the first letters of their names must be able to form some catchy acronym. Dig out some economic and demographic data on the countries you have selected, discard the pessimistic stuff and set up an investment fund. Establish a board of directors comprised of washed-up retired bankers and politicians with weak morals and time on their hands – there are plenty – and Bob's your uncle, you have your very own self-licking lollipop. You will have more investors than you can cope with. I promise.

But at least the brains behind the BRICS and the MINTS are offering up some kind of optimistic vision of what may happen. There are plenty more doomsayers predicting all sorts of apocalyptic scenarios. There are moments in Nigeria when this pessimism seems justified, and none more so than on a trip south to the oil-rich Niger Delta where the Niger river meets the sea in the Gulf of Guinea. Before it became synonymous with the production of crude oil it was a major producer of palm oil, which is why the British ran it as the Oil Rivers Protectorate in the nineteenth century. The slave coast became the oil coast. It is now one of the most productive oil-producing spots in Africa – and also one of the most polluted, disputed and fractious places you could imagine.

Port Harcourt is the hot, sleazy regional capital of the Delta region, a city of nearly two million people, devoid of any architectural, cultural or social amenity. It exists only as the functional gateway into the deep recesses of the Delta and its myriad oil production facilities. On one occasion, I was visiting some clients and colleagues who had recently been caught up in an audacious and large-scale kidnapping of oil workers by one of the region's notorious militant groups. These gangs are the Delta-equivalent of the Area Boys back in Lagos but operating under the dubious guise of sticking up for the local communities who see little of the wealth generated by the extraction of the oil from under their feet.

This visit required travelling overland with our client from Port Harcourt to Choba, a small outpost deep in swamp country, where thick, hard-to-refine crude oil with treacle-like viscosity rises to the surface in the gloopy marsh. Choba makes Port Harcourt look like Florence. But after a hazardous and uncomfortable journey to get there, you don't care. You require a police escort to travel out into the Delta. Our client had organised a police pick-up truck to drive ahead of us with an armed guard in the back. Our guard was at least seventy, a wizened, smiley old man with one tooth and one shoe – an old Green Flash plimsoll which was of similar vintage to his bolt-action Lee-Enfield rifle. He was inordinately proud of this rifle, a decades-old relic left behind by the British Empire. The fact that he did not have any ammunition to load it with reduced its likely efficacy in the event that we were to be ambushed by bandits. Bless him, he would be useless in a firefight but at least he was earning a few dollars for a day out in the countryside.

The journey takes you through mangrove forest and over creeks interspersed with small hamlets consisting of a few wood-built residential shacks and multiple churches with corrugated iron roofs. Each belongs to one in a bewildering array of different evangelical Christian denominations loudly announcing the imminent return of Jesus. Should our Lord choose southern Nigeria as the location for his next earthly manifestation, he will have his work cut out. Most of the shacks double as shops and are busy selling entirely spurious cures for AIDS.

I spent the next few days with people who had just been released after being held hostage for several months by one of the more audacious gangs, MEND – the Movement for the Emancipation of the Niger Delta. They had been held in a camp even deeper into the Delta and guarded by heavily armed, drug-taking, volatile teenagers, quite possibly with the connivance of the local authorities. Living conditions were harsh but they were not gratuitously mistreated. Indeed, one of the hostages, an amateur boxer of some note in his earlier years, passed the time teaching his captors the rudiments of the noble art, getting cross with them when they couldn't get their weed-addled minds around the finer intricacies of the Marquis of Queensbury rules. The hostages were released when some dispute over land rights, royalties and access was settled ex-judicially.

For decades, oil companies and local communities have been at war, mostly in the courtroom but occasionally literally. The rights or wrongs of their disputes have long since been lost among layers of grievance and mistrust. And what may seem from a distance like a simple dispute between haves and have-nots, has become entangled in the criminality and corruption that infest nearly every aspect of life in the Delta. From afar, it is easy to portray international oil companies operating here as rapacious exploiters of Nigeria's natural resources and often complicit in the mistreatment and degradation of the local people and their natural environment.

Close up, it never seems that obvious. There is a deceptively simple narrative of cold-hearted oil executives thousands of miles away setting out to plunder the hydrocarbon wealth of a vulnerable nation, with reckless, racist disregard for the people who have fished these coastal waters for generations. That kind of oil executive exists for sure. But the mistakes that were made were more often the result of local decisions taken without due heed of the sometimes difficult to foresee outcomes. Oil companies are traditionally staffed by mission-focused geologists and engineers. Individually, they do not imagine themselves as the proconsuls of economic imperialism. For decades, they regarded the oil business too narrowly as a series of technical challenges to extract trapped carbon from the ground. More recently, they have accepted that doing so brings intrinsic and unwelcome social and economic consequences and have tried harder (some more than others) to mitigate the obvious downsides. But by then, it was too late for the Niger Delta. The pattern of blame and recrimination was too deeply set for anything approaching a fresh start.

The workforce at any one of the many drilling, construction and storage facilities dotted across the Delta is drawn from a seemingly random cross-section of the United Nations. Thais, Ukrainians, Filipinos and many more – you name it, they were there. In a world of topsy-turvy economics, it seems it is often cheaper to hire people from the other side of the world to undertake relatively menial work rather than hire local Nigerians. It cannot really be true but that is what happens. Along with hundreds of others, they found themselves working in the oil services industry in a part of the world where nearly everything is out to make their life miserable and perilous. The suffocating humidity, the pissed-off populace, the massive malarial mosquitos – everything, it seems, is against them. They were just ordinary folk drawn to an uncomfortable job in trying circumstances, mostly because they had a family trapped in poverty on the other side of the world reliant on their repatriated earnings. In other cases, they had towering debts to repay, an unhappy relationship with the tax authorities, a disastrous credit history or steep alimony payments to meet. Either that or they were running away from something or somebody and they didn't want to be found.

There was no post-colonial fantasy pulling them to this part of Africa. This was no tented camp with crisp white tablecloths where you can quaff chilled wine while listening to lions roar and watching giraffes silhouetted against a setting sun. This was proper *Heart of Darkness* stuff. The lure was just simple economic necessity and the possibility of living your life beyond easy reach. These people often feel as if they have gone from being the foot soldiers of globalisation to becoming its casualties, without ever enjoying the fruits of their labours. They do crappy jobs in dangerous places in the hope that something better comes along. It rarely does. Everything feels compromised. The local government, the politicians, the oil companies, the community representatives, the NGOs: everybody seems tainted by decades of misrule and bad governance. It is hard to say with any certainty who is right and who is wrong in the endless arguments over culpability for the mismanagement of Nigeria's abundant natural wealth.

Leaving the Delta, you can find your spirits restored. The rest of the country has problems galore, but they often seem less dystopian and more mischievous. In 2009, Nigeria hosted the FIFA Under-17 Soccer World Cup. Nigerians are football-crazy and have done better in this tournament since it started in 1985 than any other nation. We had the unenviable role of keeping hundreds of teenagers from around the world safe and well as they travelled the length and breadth of Nigeria, playing games in front of rapturous crowds. All had gone pretty much according to plan until we got to the semi-final. On the morning of the first game, we arrived at the stadium to check all was well before the teams arrived. It turned out that, overnight, the grass had been stolen. The turf had been rolled up, put on a truck, and spirited away.

Nigeria is not without noteworthy leaders. I once spent an afternoon chatting with former Nigerian president Olusegun Obasanjo in his suite in a west London hotel. He is a remarkable man. He is a veteran of the Biafran war, a former general and political prisoner who spent three years in jail during the harsh and abusive rule of General Abacha. As president, Obasanjo was credited with helping guide Nigeria back to civilian rule and some semblance of democracy. He had genuine international stature. He is a great orator, a prolific writer and an enthusiastic polygamist.

Obasanjo has his detractors and inevitably rumours of corruption cling to him. But he can persuade you – in the moment – that all that stands between Nigeria and untold prosperity is far-sighted, selfless leadership backed up by a technocratic cadre of world-class Nigerians intent on forging a different, digital, post-oil future for a country whose wellbeing they are dedicated to safeguarding. If you point out any of the obvious pitfalls in his otherwise foolproof plan, he stares at you intently before breaking into a deep, infectious chuckle and recommending that you read one of his many long and serious-minded books on the subject. He nearly convinced me and might have totally won me over had he not – while talking to me – been simultaneously watching a TV documentary about restoring Britain's canal system and performing a detailed pedicure on his own rather long, crusty toenails.

There are public servants of high ethics and indefatigable courage who swim against the tide to improve the fortunes of their country. There are businesspeople and activists who chose not to succumb to the corrupt old order. And many Nigerians I know have decided that politics is not the answer. As a means of progress, it is redundant. Older people look back on the long years of civil war, military rule, the corruption, the failure to tackle Boko Haram and its appalling attacks on schoolchildren, systemic poverty, and the squandering of all the vast resources, mineral and human. They conclude that the politics of a venal oligarchy will never provide for a decent future. Younger people have decided that progress lies in the gaps where the state is not. The poor work in unregulated markets and the middle class opt to move away from the oil sector to pursue careers in media, fashion, film and technology. In both cases, their verve and creativity are intoxicating.

Nigeria is the product of Britain's rapid retreat from empire; a country cobbled together in 1960 by colonial rulers suddenly in a rush to dispense with an empire they no longer wanted or needed. They were in a hurry to head home. It would be hard to think of a country less designed to function effectively. Take a look at a map of the continent. Nigeria is a square block wedged into Africa's armpit. It is a hastily assembled country made up of an unholy amalgam of peoples and geographies with little obvious national, religious or cultural affinity. But a Nigerian identity has taken firm root and a vivid, brash, loud, brilliant nation has overcome terrible odds to make its mark far beyond the random perpendicular boundaries etched by imperial cartographers.

Nigerians have the enviable knack of looking forward and not being unduly trapped in their own history. But the past still lingers in the imagination. One evening, I left a Lagos bar full of foreign oil workers up from the Delta and in the mood for a good night out. Keen to avoid the consequences, I headed out to find my driver and go home. Outside, were a group of Nigerian sex workers looking for business. *Oyinbo, Oyinbo,* they called, to get the attention of the guys in the bar – the term they use for white men who may be potential customers. *Touchy toes, touchy toes,* they shouted after me as I passed by, describing the position they would adopt in order for the proposed transaction to proceed. I walked away. My driver took ages to arrive (he was probably off selling my shoes somewhere) and in those moments, standing on the unlit street corner, watching the tragedy of the women plying their sad trade, there was a poignant sense of the centuries of exploitation, from the earliest days of the slave trade onwards, that have scarred this part of the African coast. I felt the unquiet ghosts of West Africa's troubled past all around me.

The burden of my liberal conscience is of no use to modern Nigeria. There is nothing to be done to right the wrongs of the past other than to get out of the way and let Nigeria take care of itself. In many ways, this is a country ripe for revolution. It has massive wealth disparity, grinding poverty, evident corruption and criminality by parts of the ruling class who live lives of decadence and conspicuous luxury. And it has the ever-present fear of religious extremism tapping into a deep vein of latent violence. But I doubt there will be a revolution on the streets of Lagos, Kano or Abuja. Nigerians have learnt to prosper despite – not because of – their government. They know that the choice is simple: make it or be screwed.

I feel I should expose this theory to more rigorous scholarship. I should put some of what I have written here under the microscope of real-life scrutiny. One option would be to head back to Nigeria and comb the streets in search of my friend the ironing-board vendor. Together we could examine the rhythm of his daily life: getting up before dawn to spend a mostly fruitless day on the mean streets of Lagos trying to make just enough to keep him and his family in body and soul. I could then explain that he is in fact a vital cog in one of the most dynamic countries on the planet. A country that, despite the curse of oil and the mostly disastrous stewardship of the economy, coupled with the wholesale theft of the nation's patrimony, will one day prevail. That his endeavour and persistence will be rewarded. I could try that. But I think I know what would happen. He would, with every justification, drag me to the ground and beat me to death with one of his ironing boards.

10

Hide your strength, bide your time

IN 1998, A GROUP OF FISHERMEN discovered the wreck of a ship about a mile off the coast of Belitung Island in Indonesia. The ship was excavated and discovered to be just over twenty feet wide and close to sixty feet long. It was remarkably intact. Scientific examination of the ship's timbers revealed that it had been built around 830. Inside, a treasure trove of Tang dynasty gold and ceramics was discovered. This was a Chinese merchant vessel en route back to China from a trading voyage to the Middle East, twelve hundred years ago. The Belitung Wreck became one of the great archaeological finds of recent years, and scientists and historians have pored over the remarkable insight it gives us into the life and times of its crew and the world in which they lived.

We think of China now as an emerging power. We understand how its rapid growth has tilted the global economic balance towards Asia and we watch as the country starts to deploy its considerable heft in pursuing its own interests in different parts of the world. What we tend to appreciate less is that none of this is new. By some estimates, China has been the largest economy in the world for eighteen of the past twenty centuries. It was almost certainly in the number-one spot long before the Norman invasion of Britain in 1066 and did not really start to decline until the nineteenth century. The Belitung ship was just one vessel in a vast commercial fleet that plied China's trade routes in the ninth century, connecting the thriving Tang dynasty to markets around the world.

If we have failed to fully appreciate China's historical predominance, then the Chinese most certainly have not. They do not see themselves as the new ascendant power whose rapid economic growth has spring-boarded them suddenly into the superpower league and upended the natural order of geopolitical supremacy. They regard what is happening now as the reassertion of the natural order, the resumption of business as usual. This is not just a conveniently constructed narrative to justify China's more assertive and disruptive approach to international diplomacy; it is what they believe.

The scale of what China could become really began to be apparent in the years after the Tiananmen Square demonstrations in 1989, when the Chinese authorities crushed a student protest in central Beijing, incurring worldwide condemnation. The government was outwardly defiant. But the Chinese leadership under Deng Xiaoping concluded privately that their best chance of maintaining peace and compliance was to accelerate a series of economic reforms that would meet the material aspirations of people who might otherwise demand political change. That strategy has been a runaway success.

Since 1989, China has seen its economy grow 25 times in size, enjoying along the way years of over 10% growth.

The staggering upturn for China's rural poor has been the greatest escape from poverty in human history. The country now rivals the United States to be the largest economy in the world and has transformed itself beyond anybody's wildest dreams. For most of this time, the US and China have been on wary but cordial terms. Commercially, they have enjoyed a tight embrace. US consumers have bought Chinese goods by the boatload, US manufacturers have enthusiastically employed cheaper Chinese labour and Chinese companies have been on a buying spree in the US as well as tapping into the sophistication of American capital markets to fuel their ambitions.

In the background, the US was growing twitchy about China's rising power and worked hard to build a series of trading alliances in East Asia to counterbalance China's regional assumption of primacy. But there was a notion of codependency which, it was hoped, would prevent rivalry becoming hostility. This mutuality works in all kinds of ways, not least in how China secures access to oil, key to its phenomenal industrial growth. China buys oil in large part from the Middle East. America, meanwhile, has been weaning itself off Middle-Eastern oil as its own shale gas reserves became productive. It was pretty much self-sufficient in hydrocarbons by 2016. Historically, the US protected its crucial oil supply routes from the Middle East using the might of the US Navy to deter any possible attempts by Iran and others to interrupt shipments. In particular, the US kept the Fifth Fleet stationed in Bahrain to make sure the Straits of Hormuz at the mouth of the Persian Gulf were not deliberately blocked. Around 20% of the world's oil supply passes though the Straits. Nowadays, much of it now leaves the Gulf and turns left to Asia; very little turns right to the US. In order to pay for the Fifth Fleet and its other military commitments around the world, the US runs a huge deficit; a single aircraft carrier costs in the region of $13 billion. This deficit, in turn, is financed in large part by the Chinese purchasing US treasury bonds.

It is one of the absurdities of modern geopolitics. The Chinese lend money to the Americans so that the US can protect China's oil supplies to enable China to grow and overtake the US economy. It sounds crazy, but for a while it encouraged enough people to feel that this kind of intertwining of economic fortunes would provide the glue to keep the US and China, if not best buddies then close enough to avoid any unpleasantness. Somewhere in this mix was an expectation in the United States that the more capitalist China became the more likely it was that some form of political liberalisation would inevitably follow. That was wishful thinking.

Politics then intervened to mess things up. President Trump ran for office loudly proclaiming that China was eating America's lunch. The whole system, he claimed, was skewed heavily in China's favour and it was going to stop. By the time Donald Trump became president, Xi Jinping had already set China on a much more assertive course than his predecessors. Deng Xiaoping's famous dictum *hide your strength, bide your time* – by which China would play the long game and avoid unnecessary conflict or entanglement – was coming to an end. President Trump may have felt that all that was required was a noisy and histrionic tariff skirmish with China. But some of his advisers had other ideas, and in President Xi he had someone on the other side of the negotiating table less inclined to accommodate the United States and more willing to flex China's muscles. The scene was set for a good old-fashioned dollop of superpower rivalry.

The passive-aggressive politeness of before has been

replaced by much more direct and, on occasions, bellicose language. The COVID-19 pandemic (which we will come to in a later chapter) gives the dispute a sharper edge. America lays the blame for the emergence of the virus firmly at China's door. China rejects culpability and points out how much better prepared and competent China was than the US at dealing with the medical consequences. The virus may have demonstrated the massive interconnectivity between the two nations, but it also ignited public antagonism that plays well to nationalists on both sides. It is as if both countries have been playing a giant game of Twister. The dial has now stopped spinning and both sides are wondering how they can disentangle without falling over.

For foreign businesses, China is a conundrum – too big to ignore but very difficult to crack successfully. Many have done very well and have learnt how to avoid incurring the wrath of the Chinese authorities, keep their noses clean and make money. It has not all been plain sailing, even for the most sophisticated and canny of investors. In the early Noughties, a client bought up a Chinese state-owned beer maker. Like many such companies, it was over-staffed, inefficient and structured to maximise employment rather than make any kind of return for shareholders, or even brew a decent ale. They went about turning the business into something resembling a modern, commercial enterprise. This involved a painstaking series of vexed negotiations about how to reduce the workforce in a town where the brewery had been the predominant employer for generations.

The talks with the workers' representatives had reached a crunchy moment when the new management of the business found themselves confronted by an angry mob threatening violence and starting to break furniture and damage the offices.

One of my colleagues arrived to help with the negotiations, to try to defuse what had become a tense and intimidating situation. He arrived just in time for irate workers to force the management team into their office, pile furniture and machinery against the doors and seal off the plant. A few hours later and it was apparent there was stalemate in the talks. They were locked in and going nowhere – possibly for a few days. My colleague then had to make the phone call to his American wife that every Australian man dreams of making: 'Sorry darling, I won't be home this weekend; I am trapped in a brewery.'

From the outside, China can look totalitarian. But the Chinese Communist Party's grip on power is not based solely on coercion. It depends for its legitimacy on the tacit consent of the overwhelming majority of China's vast population. In turn, this requires the government to alleviate many of the pinch points – affordable housing, access to efficient local amenities, for instance – that aggravate an increasingly affluent population. They do not get it right all of the time, but officials spend a huge amount of time figuring out how to pre-empt any groundswell of popular resentment against the regime. Political freedom is non-negotiable – it is not going to happen – but the Communist Party is accountable in a way that is not always understood outside China. It is not warm and cuddly. The state can be brutal, but in its determination to remain in power it understands that to do so in a country of over one billion people you need majority consent.

Occasionally, the government will intervene directly to make the market work how it wants. For instance, if public disquiet is mounting over China's new wealthy elite being too ostentatious, then importers of expensive foreign sports cars may receive some unwanted attention. If access to affordable healthcare is causing tension, then medical suppliers may find their distribution models are under scrutiny. If the prices of industrial materials are deemed too high, then the government will find ways to have them adjusted downwards. There is less of Adam Smith's *invisible hand* of the market at work, more the heavy – very visible – hand of the Chinese regulator. If it wants to signal major displeasure, the government may well pick on a foreign company to make its point. Chinese companies also routinely find themselves in the firing line but occasionally it suits the government's political needs to make a high-profile scapegoat out of a foreign firm. Similarly, international disputes will often have domestic consequences. When China is having one of its periodic spats with Japan over who owns contested islands in the South China Sea, then Japanese companies in China may be in for a rough ride. And when the Canadian authorities detained Huawei CFO, Meng Wanzhou in 2018, Canadians in China ducked for cover.

Serious consequences await those investors who inadvertently cross swords with China's deep state, the secretive web of connections that bind together the upper echelons of the Chinese Communist Party. In 2012, Bo Xilai was the boss of Chongqing and one of China's rising political stars. He had held numerous senior jobs both in local government and in Beijing. Bo was charismatic, photogenic and popular. His career was going well. He seemed to be well-regarded, well-known and was tipped to join the elite Politburo Standing Committee. And then his world came crashing down. One of his top lieutenants and the local police chief sought asylum at the American Consulate in the city of Chengdu. They claimed to have information about the involvement of Bo Xilai and his wife in the alleged murder of

British businessman Neil Heywood.

What unravelled was an extraordinary tale of greed and intrigue. Bo Xilai was sentenced to life imprisonment for corruption. His wife, Gu Kailai was given the death sentence, later commuted to life imprisonment, for the murder of Neil Heywood. The Bo Xilai case had all the ingredients of a lurid thriller. It involved the tragic death of a man who appeared to have become unintentionally entangled in a world of political rivalry, murky business dealings and sexual jealousy. It even prompted a highly unusual statement by the British Foreign Secretary, denying that Heywood worked for Britain's intelligence service, MI6.

I was visiting the country frequently at the time. In the risk business in China, you need to be very cautious. The authorities understand and accept that you have an important role to play in guiding outside investors through China's complexities and helping them sort out some of the inevitable problems foreign companies encounter. They are not naïve about the shortcomings of the Chinese business world. But any hint that you are crossing the line into the world of espionage or acting against the interests of the state, then their tolerance becomes intolerance very quickly and with maximum prejudice. They keep a close eye on what foreign companies do in China and have also been historically wary of big international investors that short Chinese companies or openly question the validity of China's official economic data. China is one of the most naturally capitalist countries in the world and the government knows full well that they need to release these animal spirits to achieve the transformation the country requires. But it has to be their version of capitalism. They understand that the market needs freedom to generate the growth and prosperity that keeps the whole political and economic show on the road. But when someone is deemed to have overstepped the mark for whatever reason, then they reserve the right to intervene, directly and robustly. And it does not need to be an ill-prepared foreign investor, as Chinese on-line financial giant Ant discovered in 2020, when their stock market listing was unilaterally cancelled at the eleventh hour by the authorities.

It pays to be personally cautious as well. As in many places around the world, I was always conscious that my movements might be monitored in China. On one occasion, I returned to my hotel in central Shanghai after dinner. As I walked through the lobby, I had a sixth sense that someone was watching me, I felt sure something was afoot. I went up to my floor in the elevator and when I got to my room, the key card that opened the door would not work. I was now definitely concerned. I returned to the lobby to exchange the card at reception. Oddly, the receptionist seemed to know my name even before logging onto the reservation system. I got back in the lift. Alongside me, was one of the hotel's maintenance team carrying a bag of tools, a young American businessman and a Chinese student in a duffle coat and trainers. I eyed the maintenance guy suspiciously, wondering if he had just been in my room fitting some kind of device. I got out at my floor and walked purposefully to my room. Just as I was inserting the new key card, I felt a presence behind me. I turned around. It was the student from the lift.

'You want fuck?' she said in English. I hastily declined, scurried into my room and locked the door behind me. Somebody had been watching me, but not for the reasons I supposed. Of course, it is possible that the receptionist was in on some nefarious plan. That the maintenance worker really had bugged my room. And maybe the duffle coat-wearer was in fact a Chinese honey-trap, dressed unpromisingly as an oriental Paddington Bear. Possibly, she was intent on secretly filming a sordid encounter in order to extort me for some dubious end. It happens. More likely though, I was being paranoid, and they were all just trying to do their jobs and make a living. But a little paranoia is not always a bad thing in this game.

The Chinese political hierarchy presumably has had more important things to worry about than me. They are effectively performing open-heart surgery on the Chinese economy. They want to change the operating model they have relied on to transform the country thus far. They intend to wean it off the dopamine hit of big injections of public money and persuade Chinese consumers to take their stash of yuan from under the bed and spend, spend, spend like the rest of us. More technically, they want to move the economic needle from supply to demand, from investment to consumption. It is a tricky operation, and one that risks the patient arresting on the operating table if they get it wrong. It is made more complicated because they also want to reform the bloated bits of the economy still owned and managed by the state, keep the currency competitive and find a way to go green without losing any industrial momentum.

People often claim that such transitions are easier in China than, say, India because they do not have the annoying inconvenience of elections, which allows them to be more ruthless and long-term. That is partly true. But what makes the biggest difference in China is that they obsess about bureaucratic competence in a way that Japan used to, and Singapore still does. Chinese public officials face possibly the toughest exams in the world to join the civil service and politicians do their time running parts of the country far bigger than the United Kingdom before they get their hands anywhere near the main levers of national power. It is not a utopian meritocracy – nepotism and cronyism complicate matters – but it is an impressive machine and breeds some formidable and tough operators. They are not all infallible however. I once spent an unusual couple of hours with a senior official in Beijing who persisted throughout our meeting with the misapprehension that I was the Norwegian ambassador.

The sharper edge of this toughness was felt during the anti-corruption campaign that marked the opening years of Xi Jinping's presidency. This campaign was only partly about stamping out poor governance and criminal behaviour; it was mainly about asserting political control. As China had grown richer in the past decades it had also become more decentralised. Authority had slipped away from Beijing to powerful local and provincial governments run by ambitious party officials, such as Bo Xilai, keen to build their own powerful coalitions of supporters. It had also shifted to some of the large state-owned companies whose power had grown as the size and heft of China's economy soared. Chinese history has long alternated between a strong and weak centre. Xi was intent on reasserting central control, cognisant that China is often at its weakest when it lets power diffuse too far.

There was no doubt that rapid economic growth had been a breeding ground for bribery, corruption and all kinds of abusive behaviour by holders of public office. Xi knew this undermined faith in the legitimacy of the Communist Party and was prepared to take firm action to stamp out egregiously corrupt behaviour. Anti-corruption became one of his signature policies by which he would restore the party's reputation for competence. It also brought to heel those members of the political establishment with personal aspirations that might not be fully aligned with his new regime. Before the anti-corruption campaign started in 2013, there was no clear consensus on what type of leader Xi was going to be. By the time it had run its course, there was no doubt. There was a new sheriff in town, and he was here to make his mark.

The man he chose to run the campaign was Wang Qishan. Wang epitomises the nature of political power in China. Before he became Secretary of the Central Commission for Discipline Inspection (otherwise known as the anti-corruption enforcer), he had already held several senior roles, including Mayor of Beijing, where he had sorted out the SARS epidemic, and chair of the committee responsible for running the Beijing Olympics. He also ran China's financial services sector. During the Cultural Revolution, Wang had been sent to perform hard labour in the countryside around Yan'an. Here he met and became friends with Xi Jinping. They go back a long way. They know, first-hand and viscerally, the punishing consequences of what happens when the wrong people are running the country.

Wang is little known publicly outside China; he does not court publicity. He is a long-range thinker who is loyal, clear-minded and as tough as nails. There are many others like him. It is a deep bench of experienced, savvy pragmatists who can be given a fractious problem and wrangle it into submission. This is what other world leaders are up against when they deal with China. These people are not in power by accident. They have not wafted into high office on the back of dilettante roles in journalism and public relations. We may find China's new assertiveness uncomfortable. We may disapprove of how they conduct themselves and be repelled by how they treat internal dissent. But we should not underestimate their experience, their ability and their determination.

China has relied on this professional cadre of political elites to guide it through these years of enormous transformation. But it is a transformation that has been built on the hard labour of millions of ordinary workers who have toiled and sacrificed to make this remarkable economic phenomenon a reality. About a third of China's workforce – somewhere in the region of 280 million people – are migrant workers, leaving their homes, often in impoverished rural parts of the country, to seek work elsewhere and send money home to their families. They mostly exist outside the *hukou* system whereby people are registered to live and work in a specific place. When they head home each year to celebrate China's lunar new year, it is the largest human migration in history.

This floating army of workers has moved way beyond China's borders. Many face real hardship and exploitation. In 2004, I got some insight into just how tough and unpleasant the lives of Chinese migrant workers can be when working on a court case in the north of England. On the evening of the 5th of February that year, the regular cockle-pickers in Morecambe Bay on the Lancashire coast decided to call it a day and head back over the sand to the shore before the tide turned and the sea rushed in across the wide shallow bay. Further out, nearer where the waves were breaking, was a team of relatively new Chinese cockle-pickers, illegal migrants from Fujian Province. As the regulars headed inland, they shouted to the Chinese crew, alerting them to the time by pointing at their watches and then at the sea, trying to mime the rising tide. Either the Chinese didn't understand, or they felt they could gather a few more bags before they too called it a day. Either way, by 9.30pm that evening twenty-three of them had drowned, caught by the fast-moving February tide as they attempted desperately to beat the rising water and make it back to the shore and safety. Most of them could not swim and even if they had been able to, the wind and the currents would still have made the chances of survival extremely remote. They had left it too late.

The Chinese had been working on Morecambe Bay for a few months. Most of them had been smuggled to the UK in search of work by so-called *snakehead* gangs, charging them the equivalent of $30,000 to bring them the 5,000 kilometres to this cold northern corner of Europe. They were paid about $10 per bag of cockles and lived in coercive indentured conditions, mostly in nearby Liverpool. We got an insight into just how bleak their lives were when the leader of the local end of the gang was brought to trial. We were asked to explain how the whole system worked for the judge and the jury. Using state-of-the-art software graphics, we were able to reconstruct the journey each victim took from China. It tracked them from their home village along the particular trafficking route they took through central Asia and into Europe, their connections to other victims (many were related) right through to the exact point on the beach where their bodies were recovered by the coastguard.

Few people had realised the extent to which Chinese migrants were working in Britain or of the complex criminal networks that brought them to the country. As the trial got underway it became clear that there was an entire labyrinth of organised crime connections that brings agricultural workers from the backwaters of Fujian to Lancashire and elsewhere. It was a timely reminder that, for all the glitz and new conspicuous wealth on display in China's big cities, this is an economic miracle that has also taken its toll on the poorest and most vulnerable.

China's international economic impact goes way beyond the desperate lives of cockle-pickers. Xi Jinping has banked much of his prestige and status on another of his signature policy initiatives – the Belt and Road Initiative. This is a government-backed development initiative to invest in major infrastructure projects in over seventy countries around the world. The Chinese talk about it almost reverentially as a modern-day incarnation of the Silk Road, China's historic link through Central Asia that connected the country commercially to India, the Middle East and eventually to Europe. The initiative is not without its international objectors, who allege that the terms of trade are often grossly unfair, creating debt dependency in economically vulnerable countries. It is certainly a great way for China to export deflation out of the Chinese economy by shipping surplus construction capacity to countries like Pakistan, hungry for everything the Chinese want to build. Others see it as part of grander Chinese designs to project power and influence in ways that upset Western interests. The Chinese are most intolerant of what they see as jingoistic hypocrisy by former colonial powers unable to come to terms with their now-diminished status.

China does not take criticism easily. There is a prickly assertiveness in the way China now conducts itself. It is very sensitive about how it treats its own people and what it regards as the territorial integrity of Greater China. As relations with the US have become more acrimonious, it is getting tougher to be neutral. Countries like Australia have a hard time. China is its largest trading partner; the US is its key strategic ally. Keeping both happy is not easy. European countries wanting to deploy Chinese telecommunications technology risk the wrath of the US if they do so, and the threat of commercial retaliation from China if they renege on deals already agreed. Western companies with large exposure in Hong Kong dance awkwardly on the head of a pin as they find it ever harder to stand apart from the political fray. Once China may have made its displeasure known in private with a stern, behind-closed-doors verbal thrashing. It is now much more likely to deploy the new breed of *wolf warrior* government officials who show no hesitation in turning up the nationalist rhetoric, taking the fight out into the street and putting the boot in. No doubt China will still play nicely on occasion and tone down some of the harsher vitriol if that suits its specific needs. But, in the main, the gloves are off.

Bluntness sits quite naturally with many Chinese. I recall giving multiple briefings to teams in China and encouraging people in the company to ask questions. This process reveals a lot about a country. In the US, the youngest and brightest are climbing over each other to ask the smartest question and be noticed. In Germany, they want you to explain with granular pedantry how the strategic plan will be implemented over the next ten years, with a detailed exposition about how key milestone criteria have been determined. The Japanese are just mortified by the prospect of being asked to question the boss in public; it is like trying to push water uphill. In China, it is a blood sport. I recall facing a barrage of questions from young, mostly female, Shanghainese. Nobody bothers to put their hand up, they just fire away. Two questions stick in my mind: 'What do you do all day?' and 'How much money do you earn?' I had no idea what the answer was to the first one and managed to dodge the second.

On a separate occasion, I found myself in some rain-sodden woods in Shropshire with a group of Chinese petroleum engineers. They were being taught how to handle themselves in the event that their vehicle was ambushed by insurgents en route to an oil installation in Mali. Shropshire on a wet Wednesday morning in February was doubling as the southern Sahara. The students are driven by an instructor along a rough forestry track. After a few minutes, they emerge into a clearing, at which point a group of people hired for the day from the local village, jump out from behind the trees, let off thunder flashes and rush towards the Jeep, screaming abuse. Even though it is obviously a simulation, it can be intimidating. That is the point. In the main, everybody who comes on the course does exactly as they are told by the instructor, a grizzled Royal Marine veteran. They are meant to lock the door and lie as flat as possible on the back seats. Not the Chinese, they were straight out of the vehicle and getting stuck in. One poor lad, who had turned up on his day off from the local chicken farm to earn a bit of extra pocket money by being a jihadi for the morning, found himself face down in the mud with Mr Wong's boot on his neck.

Logically, we should assume that China will avoid letting this new public forthrightness spill over into outright aggression. It has come too far and achieved too much to risk blowing it now on a dangerous confrontation with the US. But it will be a tense few years. Doing business in China has always been complicated but is made even more so by talk of the world bifurcating into a Chinese trading block and a US equivalent. Yet the idea of China retreating behind a bamboo curtain seems improbable. It is just too big; it would poke out the sides. No doubt, China's accession to being the undisputed largest economy in the world will not be without some major bumps. But this is not a country that got rich on the back of a windfall surge in commodity prices, and it is no longer a country that prospers only by making things faster and cheaper than other people. It has world-class technology companies, including extraordinary artificial intelligence capabilities, given that it has the data of over a billion mostly compliant people to test algorithms on. It is proud of its heritage but not sentimental about its past. It feels its time has come.

China is a great power again. Its power and influence are facts of life however much it antagonises those in the West who feel it poses a threat to the post-Cold War hegemony. Whatever misgivings China arouses, it is back where it feels it belongs. There was a clue in the Belitung Wreck. The ship, built in the style of an Arabian dhow, is now proudly on display in a Singapore museum. Scientists have spent years since its discovery examining the construction techniques used to build the ship, identifying how and from what it was built. They concluded that it was almost certainly built in Basra in Southern Iraq, now a city awash with Chinese oil workers and a key transit port in China's hydrocarbons supply chain. They also discovered that it was built from wood sourced from forests in East Africa, another important destination for modern-day Chinese trade, investment and commerce. Normal service, it seems, has been resumed.

11

An insomniac on the Potomac

IT IS 3AM AND I AM WIDE AWAKE. It is jet lag, the occupational hazard of the frequent traveller, as usual. It is too early to call it a night and get up, but I do not feel sleepy in the slightest. I blame the hotel. When I checked in and came to my room yesterday evening, I was presented with a pillow menu. If you are looking for that defining moment at which our epoch reached peak decadence, then the arrival of the pillow menu might just be it. The moment when our actual requirements become so far detached from our perceived desires that our society can no longer support its own weight and implodes. The stage when we smash through the top of Maslow's hierarchy of needs, leaving it shattered in pieces as we flounder around looking for yet more ridiculous must-have substitutes for genuine contentment.

It could be our equivalent to the moment when an obese, consumptive, Roman aristocrat said: 'You know what we need to really get this orgy going? Linnet-tongue pâté. Oh slave, go and catch me 5,000 linnets, rip out their tiny tongues and make them into a fine pâté. And we'll have a side dish of ocelot's eyelashes while you are about it – in a light saffron broth.' A couple of weeks later and the Visigoth hordes swept through the empire and sacked Rome. It was game-over for the Italians.

Anyway, whatever combination of pillows I chose from the menu last night in my befuddled state has not done the trick and I blame the lumpen contortions of misshapen linen scattered around me for stopping me from getting more than a couple of hours of fitful slumber. We are not at our best at 3am. It is the time that counter-terrorist teams usually choose to storm buildings and release hostages because the hostage-takers are likely to be at their lowest ebb. It is also the time of day that we are most prone to those moments of quiet desperation, paranoia and self-destructive brooding. The time we obsessively replay fraught conversations in our head, frustratingly figuring out the killer riposte we should have delivered rather than the lame waffle that in reality is what we said. And, as some of us have discovered to our cost, it is not a good time for decision-making.

When I was a teenager at boarding school in the 1970s, an accomplice and I decided to start a campaign to unseat the headmaster and change the way the school was run. One night, long after the rest of the school was asleep, we wrote a lengthy, detailed letter to the headmaster, informing him of our decision concerning his future, slipped out of a window, scuttled around to his house under cover of darkness and posted it through his letterbox. That was a classic 3am move. By the time we got to breakfast, we realised that the general strike we were planning was probably not going to get the widespread support we had – in our nocturnal revolutionary fervour – presumed.

Sleeping pills are an option of course, and I am not averse to a little pharmaceutical assistance. But it is too late now, I need to be up in a few hours anyway – and sharp as a tack to be interviewed by attorneys from a US congressional committee. I look out of the window. It is still dark but there has been a perceptible lightening of the sky. There is a hint of that pre-dawn metallic grey that suggests that this long night might be drawing to a close. I abandon all attempts at sleep and decide to take one of my very favourite walks.

This wonderful circular walk takes in many of Washington's famous sights and monuments. I usually start from my hotel near Dupont Circle and head down to Lafayette Square and the first landmark on the itinerary, the White House. The streets are mostly deserted at this time so you can be pretty sure that the president's security apparatus will know you are there as you pause outside and peer through the railings to see if you can catch a glimpse of any goings-on inside. Everybody does this. They stare intently at the windows, hoping to spot something happening. What do they expect to see? The president in a late-night poker game, or jelly-wrestling with the Secretary of State?

I was once lucky enough to be shown around the White House. We were escorted around that part of the building known as the West Wing that contains the Oval Office and where the president's staff work all day and most of the night in remarkably cramped and scruffy conditions. We were accompanied by a Secret Service agent and he quickly established that I was British. Maybe this was the reason that he took an instantaneous and intense dislike to me.

Whatever it was, we soon found ourselves in the basement, with our guide pointing out some black scorch marks on the wall of the cellar directly underneath the White House. He asked if anybody knew what had caused these marks. His eyes were firmly on me. Before anybody had time to answer, he explained that they were caused when the British burnt down the original White House in 1814, his stern gaze remaining firmly trained on me the whole time, his loathing now so overwhelming he was no longer making any attempt to contain it.

'Listen dude', I said. 'We only burnt it down because you lot had just torched the city of York (now Toronto) in Canada. And frankly, you got off quite lightly. In any event, this all happened 148 years before I was born so why don't we quit the xenophobic posturing and just continue with the rest of the tour.' Actually, I didn't say any of that. I giggled nervously, looked at my shoes and scratched my nose. But at 3am the following morning that is exactly what I wished I had said.

Once you have had enough of the White House, or been moved on by the police department, head down 15th Street until you get to the National Mall, the central outdoor public space stretching westwards from Capitol Hill. First stop is the tall, Egyptian-style obelisk of the Washington Monument, the tallest structure in downtown Washington and beautifully floodlit. In the day, you can tell that two different types of stone have been used. About a third of the way up, the marble suddenly changes to a different shade from that used to construct the lower section.

The original funding for the monument dried up in 1854 and work stopped on its construction, only recommencing in 1876 when the federal government stepped in with the additional funding. The original marble came from a quarry that was no longer in operation, so they had to source marble from a different quarry near Baltimore. Once in situ the new marble's different shading became evident. Nevertheless, it is a superb monument, as well as an early indication of the continuous arm-wrestle that still goes on with the federal government over who-pays-for-what in the US.

Pause by Washington's monument and take in the scale and grandeur of the Mall, from the Capitol to the east to the Lincoln Memorial in the west. It gives you a sense of how self-confident and wealthy the US felt, to have built with such ambition on a swamp by a river. This is a country with something to say. Whether or not it is a fitting memorial to the country's first president, George Washington, is another matter. It certainly has scale and grace, but you might think it should more specifically reflect the man who led the revolutionary army to victory. There was even a suggestion in 1782 that he should be crowned King of America. An idea he angrily dismissed, so perhaps he himself would approve of being memorialised in the abstract.

I remember seeing old cine-films of my parents standing by the Washington Memorial. They first came here in 1962 and I was with them. I remember nothing about it as I was a foetal speck inside my mother at the time. In fact, it is possible that I was conceived on board a ship sailing for New York. The fact that my parents were sharing a tiny cabin with my older brother and sister still brings a grimace to the faces of my siblings nearly sixty years later.

I remember my parents talking about that first taste of the US with wonder and awe for the rest of their lives. They rarely returned and, like many Brits of their generation, they were quick to find fault with modern America. For them, it was the concept of America, rather than what they perceived to be the reality, that held their admiration. But that condescension that the British have for the US is, more often than not, to cover our own insecurity that the country we still like to feel we invented left us trailing in its wake generations ago.

When I moved here in the 1990s, America was not what I was expecting. It was more snobbish and cliquey than I anticipated. So much for the egalitarian paradise. This was a society where people expended a lot of energy trying to find divisions to split and fall out over. It could be race, religion, ethnicity, education, occupation, wealth, body-shape and, more recently, the great Trumpian experiment in visceral nativism. It was still a nation where you could arrive dirt-poor and within a generation be richer than your wildest dreams. But if you are born poor in the US from the wrong side of the many tracks that determine opportunity, it is harder than the mythmakers claim to pull yourself up by your bootstraps.

And yet for me it was like an adrenaline shot to the heart. I realised for the first time that to be ambitious is not just acceptable; it is expected. And that there is genuinely an expectation that tomorrow will be better than yesterday. In Britain, we can be suspicious of ambition, conflating it with greed and conceit. Better to underplay one's hope and capabilities than to risk any kind of failure and the consequent opprobrium. Mediocrity, for some, is a safe bet.

Back to the walk. Continue south past the Washington Memorial until you reach the Tidal Basin, a man-made reservoir edged by cherry trees gifted by the Mayor of Tokyo to the city of Washington DC in 1912. It should look beautiful in the early dawn light. The basin's natural serenity was disturbed one night in 1974 when a congressman was stopped nearby in his car by police officers. They discovered he was accompanied by an Argentinian stripper named Fanne Foxe. When the police approached, Fanne jumped out of the car and into the water and tried to swim off. This was just another example illustrating the enduring truism that illicit sexual shenanigans and male-dominated politics are two sides of the same coin the world over. Wherever men gather together to practise the dark arts of politics then the apparent compulsion to engage in inappropriate, furtive and often deviant sexual hi-jinks follows, like night follows day. Perhaps in North Korea they are all too scared to stray from the path of righteousness. But I expect even there some of them are getting up to mischief.

Sexual misdemeanours can be a show-stopper on occasions, while at others they are no barrier to achieving the highest office in the land – or at least fame of some kind. For many years we worked for Hollywood studios that were producing TV shows featuring contestants drawn from the general public. Over time, you become tuned in to the studios' distinct risk tolerance. Prospective members of the public eager to take part in the more extreme reality television shows need to be screened beforehand to find out what skeletons they may have in their closet. Normally, you would be looking to check there was nothing too embarrassing in a person's backstory, but with reality TV, some spice and minor sexual deviancy is essential.

America is at once prudish yet liberal, profane yet moralising. One of my oddest days in New York was spent in the office of a lawyer presenting the results of an enquiry into one of the attorney's New Jersey clients who had been defrauded. It turned out that the chief finance officer had stolen money from the company to pay for his penis enlargement surgery in Mexico. When the procedure went horribly wrong – he ended in a smaller state than when he started – he stole more money in order to pay for a succession of corrective surgeries. This was, of course, a pathetically sad human story, yet at the time, I confess, I just found it hilarious. I remember sitting in the lawyer's meeting room with representatives of the company's management team and their auditors. The photographic evidence was laid out on the polished mahogany for all to see. Half the room was in a state of outraged moral indignation with all the violated sensibilities of the Puritan settlers who arrived in Massachusetts in 1620. The other half were struggling to suppress hysterical laughter. One senior partner from a top accounting firm was biting his tie to stop giggling.

Just when I was sure that investigating the tumescent qualities of a deformed penis was as strange as it could get, another assignment came along that beggared belief yet further. This time the client was in California and he was on the verge of taking his wildly successful biotech company public. Before listing on the stock exchange and facing unprecedented levels of public scrutiny, he subjected himself to what is known as a reverse due diligence. This entails unleashing a crack team of researchers on yourself so that you will know in advance any potential reputational problems that will likely come to light when the media and regulators turn their spotlight on you. Politicians running for high office do it and so, occasionally, do prominent business figures. In this case, there was little of note about our client. He had, it seemed, led a largely blameless – if boring – life of hard work and commitment to building his business empire.

But there was one thing. Through a piece of near-genius research, the kind of analysis that still requires instinctive human intuition and not artificial intelligence, one fact emerged that we needed to bring to our client's attention. Telling him was to be one of the most cringingly embarrassing moments anybody could imagine. It turned out that, in a former career, his wife had been a porn star. He was silent for what seemed like an age when he got the news. Then, very slowly and without making eye contact, he politely said thank you and left. He paid our bill and we never heard from him again.

What Thomas Jefferson would have made of these kinds of antics we will never know. But he is right there on the southern side of the basin. The Jefferson Memorial rotunda is a neo-classical peach, perfect in scale and proportion. Inside, Jefferson's statue stands almost six metres tall, staring back across the water towards the White House. He was the epitome of the enlightenment, a genuine renaissance man and one of the principal authors of the Declaration of Independence, among his many other accomplishments.

He is portrayed in bronze as a model of wise and patrician countenance. He has certainly gone down in history as one of the great brainboxes of all time. President JF Kennedy said, when hosting a dinner for forty-nine holders of the Nobel Prize at the White House: 'I think this is the most extraordinary collection of talent, of human knowledge that has ever been gathered at the White House – with the possible exception of when Thomas Jefferson dined alone.' Clever clogs. My grandmother once told me that our family was directly descended from Thomas Jefferson. At the time, I had no idea who Thomas Jefferson was; he might have been the milkman for all I knew. By the time I came to understand that this might be quite a cool connection, she had died, and I never got to establish where she had got this idea from. It is possible, but unlikely, that my grandmother had heard the JFK quote and was just getting delusions of grandeur. She definitely did not know that Jefferson may well have been the father of five children with Sally Hemings, one of his slaves living at Monticello, his estate in Virginia. That would have stopped her in her tracks.

My grandmother was, both by birth and temperament, a Victorian. To father children with a slave (as opposed to owning a slave, ironically) would have been an egregious violation of her austere moral code. It would have incurred insane amounts of lip-pursing and handbag-clutching, two of her many ways of expressing extreme disapproval. Had we really been related, then that particular fact would have been locked deep in the vault along with all the other family embarrassments. It is a big vault. Jefferson's slave-owning has so far survived attempts by historical revisionists to negate his status as one of the icons of American history. As one of the midwives of the Republic, his reputation, like the constitution he helped shape, is probably sacrosanct. But the cultural wars that have scarred this country deeply in the past few years may yet erupt around the legacy of this most extraordinary of the Founding Fathers. It would be intriguing to be descended from Thomas Jefferson, although being related to somebody born in 1743 is not quite the exclusive genetic club I once thought it might be. The exponential nature of multi-generational reproductive cycles means there will be millions of us. But standing by his big bronze foot, I like to pretend I feel some affinity.

Keep walking along the cherry-tree walk around the Tidal Basin to the Franklin Roosevelt memorial. This tribute to one of the nation's very greatest presidents has been mired in controversy. The image shows FDR seated with a cloak over his legs, disguising the fact that he is in his wheelchair. This is true to life, as he did indeed go to great lengths to avoid ever being seen in public in his chair, given the stigma against disability at the time. But his greatness as the president who lifted his country out of the Great Depression and then led it through World War Two is only enhanced by acknowledging his personal physical struggles, so perhaps this monument was the opportunity to show his private as well as his public fortitude. Many feel the monument should reflect the truth. Turning north, you will reach the Martin Luther King Jnr Monument; prepare to be disappointed. The image of King is too solemn and impassive for a man of such extraordinary passion and vigour. The guy depicted in this statue did not deliver the 'I have a dream' speech. He deserves better. He needs to be standing tall, animated, and with his arms in the air. You may well notice the different racial make-up of the crowd at King's monument to the other monuments. The black-white ratio is flipped. That is not always a popular thing to point out.

The Second World War monument is worth a stop, less for its architectural qualities and more because its scale gives you a sense of what this country is prepared to sacrifice when it is roused and mobilised. But prepare yourself for what comes next: the Lincoln Memorial, the great Greek Doric temple building marking the western end of the National Mall. Approach past the reflecting pool, climb the steps and pass through the thirty-six fluted columns (one for each state of the union at the time of Lincoln's death) and there he is, Abraham Lincoln.

Now this is someone I would give anything to meet. I am not interested in going to Mars with Elon Musk or Jeff Bezos, and I am certainly not bothered about a long-weekend inter-galactic road trip with Sir Richard Branson. No, I am waiting for some teenage savant from Silicon Valley to invent a time-machine. I will be first in line. Swipe my credit card; fire it up; don't bother with the safety video; skip the in-flight meal; just take me back to the middle of the nineteenth century and drop me just up the road here in Washington DC.

In those days, ordinary people would often wander into the White House and talk to Lincoln. There he would be – this angular, scruffy, absent-minded obsessive. These days he would have psychologists falling over themselves to locate him on one spectrum or another. A cunning parliamentarian, he was a man who could – by turn – persuade, manipulate, inspire, coerce and out-think the wiliest of his opponents. That is, when he was not sitting in front of the fire darning his own socks. A dirt-poor war veteran, who dragged himself up to occupy the highest office in the land, faced the toughest presidency of them all and was then murdered at the moment he had to try to put all the pieces back together again. A modest, melancholic loner prone to introspection, who also enjoyed the adulation and limelight, whose visceral grief at the death of his son Willie he repurposed as iron determination.

As you can tell, I am a fan. His statue is magnificent but for my money he looks too calm and majestic, seated and staring back up the Mall to the Capitol. Turn to your left and there is the Gettysburg Address inscribed on the inner wall of the building, one of the most inspiring paeans to peace ever written. A model of elegant brevity. He wrote it very quickly on the train on the way to the town of Gettysburg in Pennsylvania, where the famous civil-war battle took place. It was here that he was to deliver the speech as part of the battlefield consecration after the war had ended. But to write something that brilliant so quickly does not fit with the aura of the majestic, calm figure in the memorial. Prose that brilliant, that intense, written at speed, almost certainly comes from a dynamic surge of agitated, depression-fuelled creativity, not from measured contemplation. And if you fancy yourself as a wordsmith, read it and weep. This is the master at work.

Lincoln, for all his extraordinary skills, was probably not a man of easy charm. I spent an evening listening to President Clinton a few weeks after he left office. Now here was a man of enormous charm. He talked eloquently, without notes, for what seemed like an age, explaining his recommended solution for all the great issues of the day. It was just before 9/11, when global affairs seemed much simpler and America was more at ease with its own role in a world that had not yet had the brutal awakening that was to arrive a few weeks later in September. I listened, captivated by his fluency, his easy command of detail and the way he was able to link seemingly hitherto unconnected ideas in a way that made you feel the links were entirely obvious and part of an explicable pattern of how the world worked. Later that evening, I tried to remember and retell what he had said. My mind was blank. I could not really remember anything he had said. It was all in the telling, all in the husky-voiced southern charm.

Leave the Lincoln Memorial and take the short walk to the final stop on our tour – the Vietnam Veterans Memorial Wall. Many people come to Washington just to see this dedication to the 58,000 Americans who died in the Vietnam War. It is haunting. A wall of black, reflective stone etched with the names of the dead and half-buried into the contour of a grassy slope. Half grave, half trench, it stays in your mind. When it was commissioned, some veterans resented the lack of grandeur, but the emphasis on loss and sacrifice is spot on. All the lettering listing the names of the dead are the same height – no variation for rank – and you can only read the actual names when you come close. In death, everybody is the same. From a distance, they are just indecipherable statistics; up close, they are somebody's son, brother, father, uncle, grandfather. During the day, you will see any number of Vietnam veterans, many still with evidently unresolved issues about the war. But you will also see the wider demographic of America in the tour groups that come here all day throughout the year, apart from the harshest days of winter. Like the battlefields of Flanders, it is a shrine to lost youth.

The US baffles me. It is a country that has changed me more than any other, but I cannot get past its multiple contradictions. A nation born under unprepossessing circumstances, but one that had the remarkable good fortune to be forged by a Jedi-like cohort of genius generals and statesmen. Men that conceived of a nation based on the notion that all men are created equal. Except those that are not. An omission corrected in law but a dislocation that still exposes the marrow of modern America. A nation with an unsurpassed capacity to innovate and to generate incredible wealth, but with no consensus on how that wealth should be deployed for the benefit of the wider commonwealth.

A young country that was tested by foreign aggression and then tested further by a civil war. This grievous injury eventually healed. But it is like one of those wounds where shrapnel is left in the body – the wound is stitched up and infection is kept at bay. Over time the scar fades. But below the skin, the original harm remains. Just below the surface, it itches away and then occasionally flares up, still livid. This is a country with a tendency to cleave over so many things: race, religion and its propensity to engage in foreign wars in faraway countries. Wars where the reasons for fighting, however noble or imperative they may once have been, become lost and hijacked by time.

There is a contradiction that runs through the nation's self-image. On the one hand, this is a country with a profound sense of its own collective self, a unifying American exceptionalism. If you watch American sitcoms, you get that sense of a common, comforting cultural identity. You see it in the way America fetishises its Hollywood stars, in how iconic, homegrown brand names become embedded in the vernacular and in how it builds great rituals around sports that few other nations play. America is not alone in this, but it does it on a scale and with an enthusiasm rarely seen elsewhere. By contrast, it also celebrates the rugged loner. The independent, self-contained cowboys. The rootless, nomadic frontiersmen, reliant only on themselves. Nobody describes this schism running through the heart of the Republic better than Bruce Springsteen. He may have been left out in the cold while the country's culture wars have raged in recent years, yet he remains the poet laureate of America's fractured soul.

It seems that once every generation or so, America wearies of over-reach, of seeing itself as the answer to all the world's problems. It turns inwards, seeking something of Jefferson's original vision – still deeply baked into the national psyche – of a self-sufficient federation of affiliated states distrustful of the centre and of interference from abroad. And then the cycle turns and the alternative vision of America the Great comes back into vogue, America the vehemently anti-imperial, imperial power. This seems to me to be the unresolved contradiction at the heart of the nation. As I write, this national identity crisis between domestic, mercantile America and global, superpower America is being played out most vividly and with enormous drama. It has now taken on a rarely seen intensity; it almost feels at breaking point as the Capitol is stormed by an angry mob of political agitators. It seems, from afar, like a nation divided against itself – or perhaps like two alien nations forced into unwanted cohabitation. But for most of its history, it has been a country riven with the anguish of a national identity crisis. Unity has been the exception not the rule for the past 250 years.

There were occasions when these divisions were laid bare. Hurricane Katrina hit the coasts of Florida and Louisiana in 2005 with devastating consequences, causing immense destruction and loss of life. In the days immediately after the storm made landfall, we had rescue teams all across the affected region. Most of them were in canoes, paddling through the submerged poor suburbs of New Orleans helping clients find and rescue survivors stranded by the flood waters and, in several cases, identifying the dead. At close quarters, it was hard to imagine that this was the United States. Hurricane Katrina revealed just how impoverished this corner of the country is, and how far removed the lives of its citizens have become from the American dream.

But the country still has unsurpassed pulling-power. For all its obvious problems – the fault lines that are riven through this nation – it is the most remarkable place I know. There are some things about America that appal me, and others that I love with an almost patriotic devotion. And almost everywhere I have been in the world, when people talk about wanting to leave and starting again somewhere else, the place more than anywhere else that they still dream of coming to is here, the not so United States of America.

The early morning walk has come to an end. Walk down the Mall and take 17th Street back to the White House. Washington is a small city, but built with the grandeur of an imperial capital. As you walk back to Dupont Circle, you get a sense that this is a city where power is wielded in a way you do not see in the magnificent post-imperial cities of Europe.

Senior American officials, and some politicians, often seem to have a sheen to them, a wholesome, confident robustness that signifies that they know they have real authority, and they know how to use it. When I met Henry Kissinger in his office, he was already an old man and had long since left public life. He is diminutive and stooped but he has a steely, slightly brooding intensity. It is as if there is a force field around him, as if the ions in the air were supercharged by his presence.

It is time now to head off to work, or whatever else you are going to do with your day in Washington. For me, I am about to endure several hours of being grilled by lawyers from a congressional committee investigating the deaths of American civilian contractors in Iraq. I have no direct connection with their death but, as is the way with these things, it is easy to become caught up in the side-winds of somebody else's controversy. As the employer of many hundreds of contractors doing similar work, my view on the circumstances surrounding this tragedy is sought by the committee.

It is a gruelling experience. Even when you are there voluntarily to provide additional illumination on a complex situation, you feel that you have been thoroughly filleted by persistent and insistent questioning. Heaven knows what it feels like if you are the actual object of the enquiry. But the experience captures something of this contrarian nation. Having blundered hastily into upending a country as hard to fix as Iraq, with little heed for the consequences, the US is then prepared to forensically examine in mind-boggling detail not just the reasons why but the detailed consequences of these actions.

I am not sure that any country – other than post-war West Germany perhaps – is willing to hold itself up to such scrutiny.

And yet, even in the act of such granular self-examination, you sense that the lessons are already being lost. The same mistakes can – and will – be made again. Maybe all countries are essentially recidivist – destined to repeat the same mistakes over and over and again. It is just that the US does so with enormous publicity and on a grand scale. As I leave the meeting and walk down the steps from the congressional offices, my sleep-deprived brain numbed further by clever lawyers with tricky questions, I am left as confused by and in awe of America as ever.

12

Risk, fear and the perils of prediction

RISK AND FEAR SOUND SIMILAR but they are not. In fact, they depend upon separate brain functions that are radically different from each other. Risk involves the objective, cerebral process of calculating the odds of some specific threatening event occurring. It is done by that part of the self-conscious brain that we can switch on and off. By contrast, fear is an immediate, instinctive response to perceived danger, often clouded by emotion.

Calculating risk is a logical process, one we can initiate and control. We may reach the wrong conclusion, but we undertake the process with conscious volition, using the super-logical linear part of our cognitive armoury. Fear comes from a different part of the brain. We experience fear based on stimuli that our brain processes, often without us realising it is doing so. This is the limbic system, that bit of the brain that we cannot intentionally control but is responsible for the behaviours we rely upon to survive. We know something is going on because we get butterflies in our tummy. This sensation – the *collywobbles* – is our adrenal glands hard at work ramping up the production of adrenaline. This super-drug is then sent coursing through our veins and arteries to give our major muscle groups the additional stimulant they need to spring into action. We need to be ready to decide if we will tough it out and fight or decide that discretion is the better part of valour and take flight. Either way, we need the additional chemically induced boost provided by adrenaline.

We also get goosebumps or feel the hairs on the back of our neck standing up. This is because when our early hirsute ancestors encountered a hungry predator, they would raise the hair on their bodies to try to make themselves look larger as a deterrent. We lost our body fur over a million years ago, but we respond as if we were still shaggy-haired early hominids. We do all of this so quickly we do not realise we are doing it. Go for a walk in your local park and you will see cats and dogs doing the same thing. (We assume that we are much further up the evolutionary scale than cats and dogs, but they can lick their own genitalia so perhaps we are not as evolved as we like to think).

This bio-software is ancient and brilliant. But it malfunctions. Its source code was written for cave-dwelling hunter-gatherers, not telly-watching, on-line-shopping, social-media addicts. Along the way, it seems, we have failed to download all the necessary software upgrades. We now fear things in the abstract that statistically are unlikely to ever affect us directly while we are blasé about things that regularly do us harm. Many of us are dismissive of everyday, commonplace risks like speeding cars, insect bites, heart disease, refined sugar, texting while driving, alcohol, chlamydia, opioid addiction, and skin cancer, all statistically certain to do many of us significant harm.

The two notions of risk and fear intertwine and become jumbled in our minds. We put too much trust in our response to fear and are lazy in calibrating and triaging risk. The net result is that we react very often to the wrong things. We do it individually as people and we do it collectively when we come together in business enterprises and governments. When you explain this to executives or government officials who have stuffed all sorts of odd things at the top of a risk matrix, they inevitably agree with you. They nod sagely and then stubbornly persist in worrying about the wrong things.

We also process risk in ways that are sometimes hard to comprehend. I am quite relaxed flying in an open-cockpit vintage bi-plane being buffeted by clouds and the wind. I find it exhilarating. But I really do not like going by elevator to the top floors of a high building. I can feel both my body and my mind pressing in on me. Of course, I understand that the lift is off-the-scale much safer than a Tiger Moth, but no amount of rationalisation can alter how I feel.

Many of our fears are rooted deep inside us and are the consequence of centuries of learned behaviour and conditioning. Even though the COVID-19 pandemic feels like a new and unusual assault on our lives, our reactions to it are rooted in ancient atavistic impulses. Pandemics have shaped us. They are buried deep in our collective conscience. Since the beginning of our time together on this planet – or at least since we found it more convenient to stay put in one place and grow crops and rear animals – we have feared them and succumbed to them. They are embedded in our common folklore, from our reflexive fear of rats and our 'poxy' insults to our nursery rhymes. We pay due deference to the word plague by bestowing on it the double accolade of using it as both a noun and a verb.

Pandemics have also been the crucible for great genius. William Shakespeare wrote *King Lear* while escaping one of London's frequent bouts of bubonic plague, and eighty years later Isaac Newton was sent home from university to avoid infection, giving him the peace and quiet to push on with the discovery of gravity in his parents' back garden. Maybe it is not a coincidence that both the mental torment of King Lear and the mighty physics of gravity remind us of the puny insignificance of mankind when up against the uncompromising primal power of a highly promiscuous virus.

Covid is high on the list of issues that we find hard to assess and calibrate. The result is that we tend to adopt absolutist positions – some of us paralysed by anxiety, and others relaxed and dismissive. We are doing this now over Covid and we have been doing it for years over our impact on the planet. The arguments over a changing climate are riddled with fault-lines, where contested science meets both stubborn denial and energy-sapping pessimism. The issue of what is happening to our planet may have been brought into much sharper focus, but, unhelpfully, we see it in the same way we have come to think about pandemics: through the blurred lens of competing bias and disputed data. Knowing whose knowledge to trust, distinguishing hard, cold facts from overheated opinion and having some sense of how to measure our concern feels nigh on impossible.

The pandemic has focused our minds on how to assess risk like nothing else in recent times. One minute, this new version of the coronavirus seemed to be on the distant horizon of our awareness and comprehension. We assumed that it was only going to affect people with an exotic culinary taste in bats from cities we had never heard of on the other side of the world. Before we had had time to find Wuhan on a map, it had arrived among us, now renamed, specifically and somehow more ominously, as COVID-19. It moved, reaper-like, through the ranks of our old and vulnerable, causing us to shutter our economy and disrupt the education and employment prospects of a generation of young people who, for the most part, have been medically unaffected. We will be arguing over our response for years and possibly decades. We will debate whether our actions were proportionate and rational, whether we understood the virology, if we interpreted the statistics correctly and how well we put aside our petty rivalries for the greater good. In short, we will try and retrospectively distinguish risk from fear.

Before we became preoccupied by pandemics, we used to worry ourselves to distraction about terrorism and no doubt we will do so again. By contrast with Covid, the odds of most of us being badly and directly affected by terrorists are vanishingly small. I have given endless presentations on terrorism, trying to persuade angst-ridden executives how rarely major terrorist attacks occur. The audience looks back at me sceptically, having been conditioned into collective paranoia by populist politicians and their enablers in the less-responsible corners of the media. When I tell the same audience that, by contrast, at least two of them will likely be arrested and jailed in the next few years for fraud, they think I am exaggerating and lose interest. Being the victim of a hard-to-predict random terrorist attack is awful but difficult to dodge. Deciding to commit fraud is a predetermined act of free will.

Knowing more about what is going on in the world often enables us to have more things to be anxious about. Our sensitivity to risk has been heightened. As tourists and as business executives, we can go almost anywhere. What was once the preserve of the intrepid pith-helmeted explorer or the gung-ho merchant adventurer is now readily available to many of us, either personally or professionally. And if hopping on a plane is not an option, then the miracles of the digital revolution mean we can experience it all remotely at the swipe of a finger. Pessimism, it seems, has better ocular skills than optimism when it comes to scanning the horizon.

There seems little point in turning to our political leaders to help us avoid conflating risk and fear. The gap between the two is much too temptingly fertile territory for all but the most principled of politicians to resist exploiting. We like to think that truth is absolute but very often it is what the rich and powerful want it to be. I am not sure that the current crop of political leaders is necessarily any more careless or mendacious with it than their historical forebears. Henry VIII had all sorts of spurious justifications for upending the entire political and religious establishment, when in fact he was really driven by the singular purpose of exchanging one wife for another. But today's leaders, even if somewhat lame by Tudor standards, do seem less concerned with covering their tracks than their immediate predecessors. Ignoring empirical data in favour of stoking the furnace of cheap popularity has become less a pragmatic compromise and more a badge of honour.

In this slippery, fact-dodging, soap-grasping world, in which the difference between risk and fear is often blurred, it seems to have become more difficult than ever to make sensible distinctions about what we should really be worrying about. Weaving its way through all of this is that sense that whatever power we once had over our own lives has slipped away from us. Decisions are made for us by politicians whose cultural values we find alien. Our lives are shaped by central bankers, invisible to us behind a blizzard of impenetrable data. Someone somewhere is writing search-engine algorithms that seem to know what we are thinking before we do. And now our liberty is curtailed by grim-faced epidemiologists and statisticians.

In our lifetimes, the world has undergone profound and often positive change, but for every silver lining it seems there is at least one dark cloud. It has been a period of amazing innovation, growth and advancement, but one that has left many of us fretful, bewildered and fearful of the future. It seems that as opportunities multiplied so did our exposure to risk. And, thanks to the ubiquity of social media, we are now bombarded by constant exposure to a highly selective, exaggerated version of what is happening in hitherto hidden corners of the planet, often deliberately tailored to reflect our particular preoccupations.

What we experience as individuals, we then replicate when we come together in businesses. Executive teams divide into those who *take* risks – salespeople and dealmakers, for example – and those who *own* risks – lawyers and auditors. When these two parts of the team are well-balanced, they help businesses rein in their wilder spirits while still being ambitious. But when they get out of kilter, so that one group dominates decision-making, you have contradictory forces pulling against each other. And when those businesses sprawl around the world in remote locations in complex jurisdictions, then maintaining the right equilibrium between adventure and prudence becomes even harder.

In 2010, I travelled to see a company that had just purchased a desalination plant in Algeria during the early days of the Arab Spring. Surrounded by an impoverished dead-end community that produced more battle-ready jihadis than almost anywhere else on the planet, it was a hotbed of violence and mayhem. Not surprisingly, the company had enormous difficulty getting the skilled engineering talent they required to live there and operate the plant. To make matters worse, the sea-water intake for the desalination process was about half a kilometre off-shore. The water turbulence at the point at which sea water entered the pipe would entice fish, which in turn attracted young children to swim or take small makeshift rafts out to sea to catch the fish. Tragically, every few weeks a child would be sucked into the pipe and end up mangled in the desalination mechanism.

This is what academic students of risk management call a *threat cluster*, the point at which many different types of potential problem intersect. The Zimbabwean plant manager described it in more colourful agricultural terms. When I later visited the headquarters in North America to discuss what they might do, it was hard to get them to focus on an obscure operation thousands of miles away. Nevertheless, I was repeatedly told off for violating their health and safety code by walking down a small flight of stairs without holding the bannister. When I drank a hot beverage from a polystyrene coffee cup that did not have a proper cover attached to it, they were apoplectic.

This seems like an egregious example of risks wrongly prioritised, but it is difficult to meet multiple competing demands in hard-to-manage decentralised enterprises. I remember a conversation with a British CEO of an energy company. That morning he, along with every other boss of Britain's major listed companies, had received a formal letter from the head of one of the country's intelligence agencies warning of the growing threat of Chinese state-sponsored corporate espionage. The same morning, his company had announced an exciting new tie-up with a state-owned Chinese company, a move which had won plaudits from institutional investors and a reasonable uptick to the share price. He asked me how he was meant to square that particular circle.

It feels uncomfortable to be squeezed between ever more impatient shareholders and equally demanding regulators. Some companies are brave bordering on reckless, others are prudent bordering on timidity. In part, this is shaped by national characteristics. One Danish client told me they were unlikely to need any help with their plans for global expansion into some notoriously troublesome markets. 'Don't worry', he explained. 'We are Vikings. We used to do this for a living.' On another occasion, I spent a frustrating afternoon in Baghdad with the general manager of a Korean company trying to explain why it was not a good idea to visit their facility on the Syrian border. The fact that it had been overrun by Islamic State fighters who were now using it as a marshalling yard to resupply their front line did not, he felt, seem to be sufficient justification to give the place a wide berth.

Other businesses are weighed down by a suffocating conservatism, a stifling sense of their own heritage. The onus of safe-guarding long-standing brands, risk-averse shareholders, pension funds and their own jobs and status leaves them vulnerable to rapid shifts in the market and nimbler, less-constrained competitors. Others in less stuffy types of business are often drunk on the thrill of change and transformation, Maoist in their need for constant upheaval and destruction of the past. They are addicted to taking big, highly leveraged risks, particularly – funnily enough – when they are spending someone else's money.

I have seen businesses succeed as the result of well-calibrated risk-taking. I have also seen how easy it is to fail despite all the most meticulous planning and precautions. And just to prove that the world is not fair, I have often seen the pathologically reckless prosper with apparent impunity. Very often it seems the slim distinction between success and failure is down to nothing more than good fortune. It also seems that success is less enduring. *Hero today, zero tomorrow* seems to be the new maxim, given the speed with which the most solidly constructed fortunes and reputations are reduced to rubble. Carlos Ghosn was the chairman and CEO of Nissan. He was fêted as the genius who revolutionised the car industry, an automobile deity who appeared to have the Midas touch when it came to re-writing the rules of the game for a stuffy old industry sector. And then, in 2018, he was arrested in Tokyo and facing a trial for fraud and the realistic prospect of a lengthy jail sentence in Japan. A year later, he was spirited out of Japan in a packing case to Lebanon, a fugitive from the Japanese authorities.

The difficulty of calibrating risk is made harder by the fact that prediction is so darn difficult, even though most of us have a deep-seated compulsion to speculate endlessly about what is going to happen. The old Danish proverb – *it is difficult to make predictions, particularly about the future* – should be tattooed on your retina if you ever fancy a job in the risk business. Of course, it is sometimes tempting to fall into the trap of being certain about what is going to happen next, particularly when an impatient client is expecting clarity and conviction, not caveat and conjecture. But it is nearly always an error. The celebrated Canadian American economist, JK Galbraith, famously said that the only function of forecasting is to make astrology look respectable. It certainly seems to get harder to understand the rhyme or reason of what is happening in the world. On the day I wrote these words, a tragic record was set when 3,000 Americans died from COVID-19 in US hospitals on the same day, yet the Nasdaq stock index hit an all-time high.

Even when you are close to the action it is easy to get it spectacularly wrong. I learnt this the hard way. I visited Tripoli in Libya shortly after the overthrow of Colonel Gaddafi in 2011. Air travel was closed so we took a taxi over the border from Tunisia. Gaddafi was still at large somewhere, hidden by his former henchmen. He was captured a few days later in Sirte and shot when he emerged from hiding in a drainage pipe. Nevertheless, it seemed like happy chaos. There was a sense of euphoria and optimism. The economics seemed to be shaping up nicely. A big country on the very edge of western Europe with vast oil reserves and a tiny population. There was little hint of religious extremism. In the late September sunshine, the Mediterranean coastline dotted with beautifully preserved ancient remains was stunning.

I visited Sabratha, a few kilometres west of Tripoli on the Mediterranean coast, and home to one of the most magnificent extant ancient theatres in the world. It was once one of the main cities of Roman Tripolitania. The site was officially shut because there had been fierce fighting in the immediate vicinity. But the sleepy guard at the gate was soon persuaded to let us in once we explained that we had come all the way from London. His only lamely expressed proviso was that we do not steal anything. We reassured him and he went back to sleep. On a beautifully warm day, wandering alone amid the glories of the Roman empire overlooking the sea, it was easy to assume that all would be well in post-revolutionary Libya, where even the revolutionaries seemed languorous.

That evening I got chatting with one of the militia members in my hotel. He was sporting the full Che Guevara chic. Beret slouched over long curly hair, ammunition belt slung diagonally across his upper body, combat-beige shirt unbuttoned to reveal gold medallions nestling in his chest-hair and mirror sunglasses worn indoors. He was a sight to behold. It turned out he was British. He had just arrived from Manchester, home to one of the biggest Libyan expatriate populations.

This was his first day as a revolutionary. He had, as they say, all the gear but no idea. The week before he had been fitting new exhaust pipes at a drive-in repair centre on the outskirts of Manchester. He had decided that he had had enough pandering to ungrateful Mancunian motorists in rain-sodden England and would try his hand at being a revolutionary in the country where his grandmother had been born. It all seemed quite comical and I confidently predicted that the country would all settle down soon.

We stood in the crowd outside Gaddafi's former palace and watched a mob of mostly children clambering up its upper stories, destroying it brick by brick even though it was on fire. The crowd was heavily armed and firing repeatedly in the air in celebration. It might have been a health-and-safety nightmare, but there was no sense of malice or aggression, just a palpable sense of joyous release. I was taken in by the romance of the revolution, by the improvisation and the sheer charming amateurishness of it all. I could not have been more wrong. This fragile state had no means to maintain law and order, and Libya's chances of a peaceful transition to a more prosperous and happier future crumbled to dust almost immediately after this visit.

History is littered with dramatic reversals of fortunes. In

1150, London was the unsanitary, plague-ridden home to a mere 20,000 inhabitants, huddled on the northern bank of the Thames. At the same time, a few hundred Algonquin people were gathering clams along the muddy shores of Long Island Sound on the heavily wooded island of Manhattan. Meanwhile, on the other side of the world in Cambodia, Angkor Thom, home to the Angkor Wat complex, was very probably the largest city in the world, with a population close to one million people. This was the capital of the Khmer empire, an established metropolis with well-ordered town planning sustained by a complex irrigation network and a sophisticated social structure.

And then, around the beginning of the seventeenth century, for reasons that are not entirely clear, the empire crumbled, and the city fell. It may have been a combination of foreign invasions from neighbouring Vietnam and Thailand, the effects of climate change, or even because the population had switched between Buddhism and Hinduism with such bewildering frequency that they had become disoriented and just lost the will to carry on. Within a generation the jungle had reclaimed the once great city of Angkor Thom. Go back even further and imagine a community of content Neanderthals somewhere in a verdant valley in what we now call the Middle East. They are scavenging for honey, picking figs from the tree, raising their children and looking after their old and sick. No doubt their life had its brutish moments, but it was also probably more bucolic than we might imagine. Then, one random day, a scouting party of adventurous, aggressive homo sapiens appears over the brow of a Lebanese hill and looks down covetously into the Neanderthals' valley. Hot and dusty after their long march from East Africa, they decide that they – not the resident

Neanderthals – are going to enjoy the easy pickings of life in the Levant 40,000 years ago.

Our more recent past is dotted with major events we seemingly did not foresee, from the collapse of the Soviet Union to the Arab Spring to the global financial crisis and the rise of populism. Many of us like to appear wise after the event but our ability to predict the big game-changers is not very good. We reassure ourselves by explaining them away as so-called black swans, the term used to describe an event that comes as a surprise, which we then rationalise with large dollops of hindsight. Designating something as a black swan lets us off the hook, excuses our failure to think hard enough about what the future may hold.

COVID-19 was not a black swan. It was very much a white swan. In fact, it was a huge, brilliant white, ultra-white, sunglasses-requiring dazzling white swan that had been flapping its wings and honking loudly for ages. Black swans do not exist in our imagination until they suddenly land among us, to our amazement and consternation. We may think that the coronavirus did just that. But it did not. It had been agitating insistently to get our attention for a long time.

In the past few years, we have seen plenty of Covid's obnoxious cousins: SARS, MERS, avian flu, H1N1, Ebola, Zika, HIV. Each has caused enough havoc and misery to make it clear that large-scale contagion is a real and present danger in our inter-connected, globalised world. Anywhere on the planet is pretty much only 36 hours away from a major international airport and there is nothing a virus likes more than frequent-flyer points. Lurking in the recent past is the ferocity of the great Spanish flu outbreak of 1919 with its 50 million victims, overshadowed in our historical perspective by the ironically far less deadly First World War.

We cannot say we were not warned. We blithely ignored it for as long as it was only affecting people on the other side of the world. But then we were shocked when it made landfall near to home. We claim to understand its clinical pathology but then stumble over the jumble of statistics. We are reckless with our own and others' health then give in to paranoid overreaction. We are impatient and then stoic, selfish then altruistic, hard-hearted then compassionate. We are too trusting one minute, too cynical the next. We reveal our worst, basest shortcomings, and then find reserves of incredible fortitude we never thought we had.

Pandemics have been a known, documentable threat for many years. A threat that has increased with global connectivity. Yet we have, for the most part, decided not to overly concern ourselves with their likely impact. We have stood by while governments have deprioritised research and preparedness. We have built taut, complex international supply chains, strung out around the world and so finely calibrated they have almost no flex when suddenly disrupted. Fine if it is table-ripe avocados, not so good if it is respirators.

There is however a clear beneficiary of our failure to discern the future and risk more accurately. It is human progress. Think back to our hairy ancestors with their fur standing on end and their tummies fluttering when they get lost in the woods at night. If someone had sat them down and gone through a detailed risk assessment before setting off on a mammoth hunt, they would have decided to stay home to eat grubs and drink from muddy puddles. Hunting mammoths would have been insanely dangerous. But mammoth hunting offered the chance of something better: comradeship, esteem, protein, sex, prestige and the fear-mitigating euphoria of collective triumph. If we really knew what was coming down the road towards us, and quite how perilous it might turn out to be, we would be reluctant to get out of bed in the morning. We would not start so many businesses, make new inventions, start crazy relationships, have children or, in my case, write this book.

13

Flying home

ON MARCH 31, 1944, the British Royal Air Force bombed the German city of Nuremberg. A place famous for hosting many of Hitler's mass rallies before the war. The raid was a failure. The bombers missed most of their targets and only inflicted very moderate damage on a city that had already been repeatedly attacked since the air campaign against Germany got underway in earnest in 1942.

In that one night-raid, the RAF lost 96 aeroplanes, resulting in the death of 545 aircrew. A further 157 were shot down and captured. It was the single biggest loss ever suffered by the RAF. These gruesome statistics added to an already appalling casualty rate for the bomber crews charged with attacking German cities. By the time the war finished the following year, 55,573 men from Bomber Command would have lost their lives. That is 44% of the 125,000 men who flew as part of the British bombing campaign throughout the war.

Nearly half of them died. Not in one ill-fated, high-stakes clandestine mission that went spectacularly wrong, but systematically and publicly, month after month, year after year. Nowadays such a sustained casualty rate would be impossible to even begin to justify. As a member of Bomber Command flying in a RAF bomber you were more likely to die than in almost any other British military activity throughout World War Two. And the civilian losses inflicted on German cities by Allied bombing were truly appalling, and on a scale that is hard to imagine. They remain a source of controversy.

Life for the British bomber crews was a peculiar mixture of contrasting emotions. In theory, they were expected to fly every second night. But very often bad weather or the complexities of scheduling and targeting meant they went several days without flying a bombing mission – what were known as *war-ops*. During these down-times they had little to do other than relax. They were able to go to the pub, go dancing and enjoy a bucolic and, by the austere standards of the time, somewhat hedonistic life in the countryside of eastern England. They had an almost inviolate hero status. They were largely unconstrained by squadron discipline. Misdemeanours went unpunished because the RAF now had more planes than crews and was reluctant to impose any sanction on men they needed in the air as often as possible.

When the weather was clear, a battle order would be posted, and they knew they would be flying that night. They would be called into the briefing room at their squadron base in the late afternoon to be given the details of their target. The men would groan if their intended destination involved flying over Germany's industrial heartland of the Ruhr, heavily defended by the Luftwaffe and anti-aircraft batteries. They would groan further if the weather forecast was for clear skies, making them easier targets for Germany's air defences. A final cup of tea, and they would climb aboard a narrow, unpressurised aluminium tube powered by four massive Rolls Royce Merlin engines. Weighed down by a huge bomb-load, the planes would lumber into the air before setting course for their target destination. Ahead of them was a cold eight-hour round-trip – or longer if they were going deep into eastern Germany.

Crossing the English Channel, they would be required to turn their navigation lights off to avoid detection by German fighters and anti-aircraft defences. Often chaos would ensue as hundreds of planes flown by boys barely out of their teens tried to avoid colliding in the gloom. As they approached the target, they would often see the flames from yet another devastated German city already engulfed by fire from repeated bombing. They would also see other aircraft being shot down and, all too often, planes crashing into one another as they struggled to fly straight in such crowded skies. From the cockpit, they could see men falling past them – just a few feet away, in some cases – as they bailed out of stricken aircraft that were going down in flames. Sometimes their parachutes would open; often they would not.

Once over the target, the bombs would be released, and the captain would then set course for the return journey. The moment the bombs were dropped, an on-board camera would automatically photograph the target over which the bombing had occurred. Marker flares were dropped in advance to designate where the bombs should be aimed. If these flares were not visible in the photograph, a formal investigation would be launched. A board of enquiry would determine if the crew had deliberately dropped their payload well away from the designated zone in order to avoid the obvious dangers of the targeted area. If they had, they would be court-martialled.

Refusal to fly also led to instant dismissal. Men who had flown multiple sorties, brave beyond measure, would on occasions just not be able to carry on, no longer able to maintain the enormous emotional burden of cheating the gruesome probability of not coming back. The RAF was tough in its deterrence. If you refused to fly, you would have your papers stamped with the initials LMF – *lack of moral fibre* – and be ejected from the service in disgrace. PTSD was a well-documented condition by then but there was only little scope for medical mitigation or leniency.

Once the bombs had been dropped, the aircraft were lighter and able to fly faster on their way home. But they also faced the constant concern of running out of fuel, particularly if the aircraft had been struck by enemy fire or suffered some kind of mechanical failure. Damaged, slow-moving planes – sitting ducks for the Luftwaffe's Messerschmitt ME109s – were nursed back across the North Sea by exhausted crews, often taking Benzedrine tablets to stay alert. They called them *wakey-wakey* pills. After they had landed, the crews would be debriefed, a glass of rum and a packet of cigarettes laid out for each man on the table in the same briefing room in which they had received their target instructions the evening before. Debriefing over, they would have breakfast and head off to get some sleep, quietly noting from the empty beds which of their friends and comrades had not been as lucky as they had that night.

This was extreme risk-taking. The odds of surviving unscathed were so low that seasoned veterans as well as rookies would, on occasion, self-harm to avoid having to continue flying. It was risk-taking not undertaken as a spontaneous, instinctive response to imminent danger but as a premeditated routine activity that was part of an institutionalised public policy of industrialised warfare. It was both statistically risky and viscerally fear-inducing. This was no conflation between risk and fear. It was both.

A few weeks after the Nuremberg raid, my nineteen-year-old father started his operational flying in an RAF Lancaster bomber. He survived horrible odds through to the end of the war, came home and married my mother. He had volunteered to fly (Bomber Command only took volunteers), presumably in the knowledge that what he was about to embark upon was extremely dangerous. He might not have known the cold, harsh statistics about quite how perilous it was going to be, but he would have known enough to understand that he would have been much, much safer doing something else. His Irish father – my grandfather – who had volunteered for and fought in World War One and had been injured at the Battle of the Somme, thought his son was nuts and advised him to fail his medical.

In the fifty-three years I knew my father, I never managed to persuade him to discuss openly why he was prepared to engage in such extraordinary premeditated risk-taking. I am not sure he would have known what to say if I had. For most of his post-war life he had no interest in talking about his military experiences. Not, I think, because of any continuing personal trauma, but because he always believed in looking forwards, not backwards. He was critical of other veterans who spent their time excessively reminiscing about their war-time service.

He would talk somewhat about the mechanics of how the planes worked – he was a flight engineer – and tell us funny stories of life on an East Anglian air base. But he spoke very little about the actual experience of aerial combat, and certainly never discussed his motivation for signing up, other than to joke about the superior pay and conditions afforded to bomber crews. We tried to get him to be more forthcoming. But he was, of course, from a generation and background that did not talk easily or readily about personal matters.

It is easy now to characterise this generation as being emotionally repressed. We live in an age that no longer believes in bottling up how you feel. We have come a long way in de-stigmatising mental health issues and promoting the value of openness and candour. That must be a good thing. He came from a different tradition. One that saw virtue in emotional containment and felt that to do otherwise was an unhealthy form of self-indulgence. If absolutely necessary, he would reluctantly discuss something personal, but only while taking the dog for a walk. And he was unfailingly modest about what he had done during the war. By contrast, had I done what he did, I would have wanted my own TV show.

In his early nineties, when he knew he was dying, he started to talk a little more about the war. But by then his memories were more fragmentary. He was exhausted by a long life and the cancer in his lungs. He was not able to concentrate for long, certainly not enough to cope with the sustained interrogation from his sons once we realised he might be about to open up on a subject that had always fascinated us but on which he had been reticent for so long.

But I think we know why he chose to fly. He had grown up a bright, ambitious, restless boy in a very poor family in a quiet provincial town. His older brother was away fighting in the Royal Navy. He craved the excitement and probably the glamour of doing something beyond the ordinary. He had also probably noticed that a Bomber Command uniform had a certain aphrodisiac pull. He would have seen other airmen home on leave and realised that in the wartime pubs and dance halls of northern England, a set of air force wings acted as a magnet for all sorts of recreational activities that a teenage boy is interested in experiencing. But once enrolled and trained, other motivations took over. There was a momentum of camaraderie and purpose that swept nearly everybody along. And once they started flying, the crews were bound together by mutual dependency that nearly always overrode individual fears and anxieties. Patriotism and duty, I think, were distinctly secondary motivators.

My father's wartime experiences – even though he did not talk about them – gave him an inner confidence. He knew he had moral fibre. I think it also gave him a clear set of criteria, an ethical framework, by which he could judge the world. He had been engaged in an existential struggle between good and evil and had come home on the winning side. I remain inordinately proud of him, long after his death. But I do not have the same grounded, deeply wired certainty about how the world operates that he had. It feels infinitely more complex, contradictory and ambiguous to me.

When I was a child, my father gave me a book entitled *Great Britons*. It was a series of short biographical pieces on the people who had not only built and shaped Britain but, it seemed, had been responsible for everything good that had ever happened in the world. They were all white men with the exception of Queen Boudica, or Boadicea as writers of the time insisted on misnaming her. She was the leader of the Celtic Iceni tribe that led an uprising against the Roman forces occupying Britain in AD60. She then spent a few years on a Tarantino-style rampage across southern England, massacring anybody with Latin GCSE. But given her martial prowess, the authors of the book had clearly decided to treat her as a kind of honorary man – or an accidental woman.

It was a reassuring version of global history from a very specific perspective. Walter Raleigh discovered the world, David Livingstone converted it to Christianity. Winston Churchill rescued the world from the Nazis, Alexander Fleming saved it from horrible infections. All other nationalities and races were either the delighted beneficiaries of Britain's munificence or unenlightened savages who had to be put to the sword. A psychotic, pathologically violent opium addict like Clive of India was portrayed not as a venal plunderer but as the bringer of good governance and law and order to a grateful India. It was a cracking good read and a beguiling, comforting account of how Britain had been the great civilising force in the world. It was, of course, complete nonsense.

Britain has a pathological need to constantly construct a sentimental, heroic backstory. A series of nostalgic narratives that define the country in the mythology of former glory. We have leaders aplenty who are adept at rewriting the past for their own ends. If I see one more movie about Britain's dogged resistance in World War Two, I will build an air-raid shelter in the garden, stock it with tins of spam and pineapple chunks then lock myself in it, never to emerge. This is not a lack of patriotism or pride in our parents' generation; far from it. It is a plea for my generation to stop trying to find the future in the forms of the past, to stop clinging to the dimly reflected valour of our forebears. It was their moment of heroism, not ours.

Growing up, my own heroism and valour seemed in short supply. In fact, I was scared of almost everything: cows, nettles, the dark, my Latin teacher, Brussels sprouts and, most terrifying of all, the *Doctor Who* theme music. Some of these things trouble me still. But after so many years in odd parts of the world, my innate timidity has been a near-constant visitor to the character chiropractor. It has been pummelled, yanked, twisted and stretched with extraordinary regularity, to the point that I can now just about make it bend to my will.

These days I can pretty much leave the house in the morning without being petrified. I am mostly confident that I will not end up being chased by a herd of rabid ruminants into a bed of vicious stinging nettles and then be force-fed cold greens by Miss Cox with the lights out. I may not be Indiana Jones, intrepid and fearless in the face of peril, but I no longer need to hide behind the sofa when a dalek appears on the screen.

If the past was a place packed with all sorts of fears – real or imagined – it at least had the virtue of apparent simplicity. As a child, when I was not hiding behind my mother's skirts, the world I could see seemed a simple if fearsome place. I thought I understood how it worked. Mostly, it divided into good and bad. Britain was good and the rest of the world was...well...foreign. Leeds United was the best football team in the world, everybody else's team was rubbish. The Rolling Stones was the greatest band ever; all the others trailed far in their wake.

That was the important stuff. On a more trivial level, politics cleaved conveniently between left and right. On the left was Harold Wilson, pipe-smoking and seemingly avuncular. On the right was the pompous popinjay Ted Heath. I knew nothing about them or their politics, but everybody seemed to agree that they represented a clear, logical choice. Over in America, John F Kennedy was the dashing war hero who saved the world from nuclear Armageddon during the Cuban missile crisis, even if some aspects of his private life were a bit fruity. By contrast, Richard Nixon was evidently a bad egg. There was a regular symmetry to how things were; they were either one thing or the other.

When I was young, I assumed that as I grew older, I would become more confident and more rigid in my beliefs, more certain and conservative, entrenched in my opinions and convictions. Now, I am not so sure. As I get older, I almost feel that life has gone into reverse. In my twenties, I felt flush with optimism, embarking on different jobs in an age when careers and home ownership were mostly available to those who wanted that predictability. In our thirties, many of us were absorbed pairing up and, for some, having kids. And in our forties, most were head-down, working hard to try to play the cards we had been dealt with as much skill and luck as we could muster.

Now, as we approach our sixties, few of us have escaped unscathed from the fickle hand of fate. We have all taken a few knocks. It seems that many of us face a growing chasm between whatever material security we have managed to cobble together on the one hand and the fissures in our sometimes-fragile emotional wellbeing on the other. Growing older is not living up to its billing. It does not feel like the benign accumulation of knowledge and judgement. Instead, it feels subtractive. Rather than age being the process of building cumulative layers of wisdom, it feels like the opposite.

This is not as depressing as it sounds. Each new year is an opportunity to shed complicated unworkable theories about how the world works. There is something strangely liberating about stripping out the old neurological wiring, heaving out the avocado-coloured bathroom suite of misconception and discarding all this unwanted mental ballast. I am eagerly anticipating that moment when I have whittled down what I know to a nice, fat, comfortable zero.

I am, though, nostalgic for that youthful luxury of certainty. I remember seeing the world with total clarity. We saw ourselves as captains of our own ship, embarking on a voyage into a world that was clearly mapped in our heads. I feel as if that sureness has drained away. Nothing is ever as it seems from afar. My adult life has broadly coincided with the time that this corner of the Western world emerged from the Cold War feeling pretty smug. We were confident our version of history had prevailed. A few decades later and that sense of destiny has unravelled in hubris, unable to withstand the barrage from the convulsion of political and social norms unleashed in the first two decades of this century.

Up close, the world is curious and baffling. In some ways, I am envious of people who stayed home, living out their days near where they were born, with their roots firmly in the *terroir* of the deeply familiar. To head out into the world, visit new places, get to know different peoples and countries is supposed to broaden your horizons. Spend time away from home and your assumptions are challenged, your prejudices exposed – or so the theory goes. To understand that not everything is how it seems, and that different points of view spring from radically alternative beliefs and experiences, must surely be better than viewing the world constantly through the same simplistic lens. But it can also leave you feeling unmoored – marooned even – adrift from that cosy sense of an ordered, logical world in which everything has its place. No wonder, then, that so many mendacious politicians trade in the fake simplicity of nationalism and spurious patriotism.

These days, my own impulse to take risks has been blunted after all those years roaming the world witnessing people in peril, seeing and occasionally experiencing the consequences. That is an itch I no longer need to scratch. I am chastened by witnessing other people's suffering. And I am dumbfounded and sometimes repelled by extreme activities that gratuitously dice with death. I know emergency-relief workers, soldiers and war reporters who have become inured to other people's suffering, to seeing the personal consequences of risks taken. They have all seen far too much, certainly far more than I have, and it has left them emotionally numb – stunted, even. They often recount their own experiences as if they are talking about someone else, as if they need a kind of third-person buffer. I have never felt that. Extreme poverty, suffering and cruelty leaves me unsettled and insecure. The terrible lives of Colombia's street children, up close and personal, is etched into my memory. So is listening to the tape-recorded voices of kidnap victims in Afghanistan pleading for their lives, or seeing the wide-eyed terror on the faces of hostages in Syria who know they are about to have their throats slit. And listening to Gerry and Kate McCann struggling to retain some kind of dignity and composure as they talked about the disappearance and almost certain abduction of their daughter Madeleine in Portugal. The list goes on.

To take risks deliberately and for pleasure seems almost pornographic by comparison. But we do it. We do so even if there is part of us that questions whether we should. As we have seen, risk-taking is the life force that urges us on, but there are times when it seems to have lost a sense of proportion to its purpose. Maybe by actively seeking the frisson of danger, we are somehow disrespecting those who have no choice but to confront extreme jeopardy, often with tragic consequences. Face to face with the stark pain of someone else's acute distress, it feels wrong. Instead, we should be grateful for our security, not tempt or taunt capricious fate. But when that moment passes and the righteousness fades, I know that many of us will take all sorts of risks to add some kind of spice into our lives. We may drink too much, take drugs, drive fast cars, go down potholes, scale mountains, ski down them, swim with sharks and voluntarily jump out of aeroplanes or off cliff edges.

We do this, it seems, because there is something missing in our cosseted lives. As our collective selves, as societies, communities and companies, we have become risk averse. But as individuals it seems, many of us have not. We need to fill the void left by our retreat to safety. For centuries, fear was a constant in our lives and for many it was an accepted part of the natural order. We have been long addicted to the narcotic stimulant required to respond to urgent fear. No surprise then that the amygdala, the almond-shaped mass of grey matter deep inside our cerebral hemisphere, still itches for a neurotransmitter with regular hits of dopamine, norepinephrine, adrenaline, glutamate, aminobutyric acid and serotonin. It is that paradox that threads through this book. By succeeding in making our lives safer we have stimulated the need to make ourselves unsafe. Not surprisingly, we are the only adult mammal that does this.

I realise now that I have been an observer not a participant. I have always felt myself to be on the outside looking in. And however fascinating or affecting my various journeys have been, I have always felt in some way that I should not have been there. I have been the grateful beneficiary of a serendipity that has enabled me to see and do what I have, but I have also felt like an interloper into other people's stories and dramas. I have been fortunate to have been where I have and to have met so many interesting people, but all the time

I felt that at any minute someone was going to tap me on the shoulder and say there had been a terrible mistake and order me home with my tail between my legs. I now know that this is what people mean when they talk about *imposter syndrome*, the psychological term that describes that persistent sense of feeling out of your depth, doubtful of your own ability and experiencing the fear that you will be unmasked and sent home in disgrace.

This used to bother me. And then I realised that I have always been an imposter; I just did not know it was a syndrome. I am pretty sure I felt it when my mother first took me to a playgroup with other toddlers. I certainly had it when I joined the cub scouts and at every school I attended. It was there at university and in each job I have had since. I feel it when I meet a new group of people and when I have to give a speech. I feel it writing this book. It has eased over time, but it is the subject of the only recurring dream I have. I now understand that this feeling of inadequacy is what energises me, gives me the drive and impetus to do things better than I might. It has oddly sustained me for decades and allowed me to live a life I never expected.

One such moment was in early 2004. I found myself on board a RAF C-130 Hercules, flying between Basra and Baghdad shortly after the invasion of Iraq by the American-led coalition that deposed Saddam Hussein. I was inside the main cargo hold where military vehicles and equipment were being transported. I was belted into the webbing that is strung along the inside of the fuselage, close to a Land Rover that had been strapped down in front of where I was sitting. Every time we hit a pocket of turbulence in the hot desert air, it jumped clean into the air, upwards and towards me in an alarming fashion, straining at its flimsy-looking restraints.

Approaching Baghdad in those days, there was the threat that the plane might be hit by missiles fired from the ground by rebel militias at incoming aircraft during their descent. The pilot took evasive measures to make it harder for the plane to become a target. He flew the Hercules as if on a very tight slalom course, banking the aircraft downwards in a series of sharp alternating spirals. The crew also fired flares laterally from the aircraft to counter any heat-seeking missiles that might be aimed at the incoming flight from the ground. The idea is that any inbound missile would follow the heat of the flare instead of the heat generated by the plane's engines. Luckily, they tell you before they fire the flares, as you suddenly feel a burst of intense heat inside the plane when they do.

Sitting there feeling apprehensive and slightly nauseous, I made a mental note to tell my dad about this flight. Thinking about him, I started to recall some of the few memories he had shared over the years of what happened on an operational mission. Ahead of reaching their target in Nazi Germany, it had been his job to release *window*, a radar countermeasure comprising millions of strips of aluminium foil fired from the plane. They were designed to blind enemy radar sets and make it harder for the Luftwaffe to detect them. And when they did come under aerial attack, they would also use similar sorts of evasive flying measures to those we were using that day over Iraq.

As they mostly flew at night, they feared being illuminated by multiple searchlights, and effectively blinded. This was known as being *coned* and it normally meant that you would be shot down. If they were coned, the pilot would adopt a flying technique known as *corkscrew*, a more extreme version of what our pilot was doing all those years later on the approach to the Baghdad airfield. This involved a high-speed twisting dive of over a thousand feet, which would generate sufficient G-force to rip the wings off any pursuing fighter and hopefully break out of the beam from the tracking searchlights. How a novice pilot in his early twenties was able to do this at night in crowded skies, gripping the manual controls of a 25-ton fully loaded bomber while being fired at is hard to imagine. Maybe that was the point, that only young men with little experience of life and few ties would be prepared to do it.

It was a strange feeling. For the first time in my life, it occurred to me that I was doing something that gave me a sense of what those crews endured. I anticipated that I would feel some greater affinity with my father and his wartime comrades. I did not. I felt fraudulent. For sure, I was on board a large four-engine war-plane flying over a hostile land with any number of militia groups actively intent on shooting down a coalition plane. But nearly all my fellow passengers were dozing. Mostly soldiers, aid workers and the odd foreign correspondent, they were evidently less excited than I was at experiencing what the pilot had described as a 'sporting' landing. They knew that the odds of us being hit were very low indeed. It was one of those moments, rather like the time in the mountain cave in Kenya, when you are eagerly anticipating some kind of emotional surge that does not arrive.

An experience that I hoped would give me insight and empathy only served to make me feel more remote. And this has been a consistent theme of spending so much time on the edge of other people's anxiety. I have led a voyeuristic life. Proximity to other people's peril has not rubbed off on me by making me more reckless and incautious. I have been fortunate beyond my wildest dreams to see so much of the world. It has been an utter privilege and I thank my lucky stars for all of it. The experience has left me with an enduring curiosity for what makes people tick and what motivates them to act as they do. But it has not left me addicted to danger. Rather, the opposite has occurred. It has made me feel more aware of my own limitations. A whiff of cordite and I am keen to count my many blessings and fly home.

Acknowledgements

This book started life as a blog when I was CEO of Control Risks. The blog was designed to share observations and experiences with the several thousand people in the company who live and work all around the world. I was urged by various colleagues, past and present, to turn it into a book after I retired. Among them, Eddie Everett, Hannah Kitt, Toby Latta, Nick Allan, Denise Kemp and Boris Starling were particularly encouraging, as was Jason Chaffer at Manchester Square Partners.

Control Risks quite rightly attaches great importance to objectivity. It aims to provide clear, balanced advice, free from personal opinion or bias. Having handed in my badge and stepped away, I have allowed myself the indulgence of recording more of my own views and beliefs than I ever did when I was running the company. All the judgements, criticisms and affections in the book are mine alone.

I am indebted to the three board chairs I served with –

Jonathan Fry, Crawford Gillies and Irene Dorner – for their guidance on how to run Control Risks. Of the company's founders, I am particularly thankful to Simon Adamsdale and Peter Cheney for putting their faith in me.

I had never written a book before and I realise now that it is hard work. I am very thankful to Simon Edge, Dan Hiscocks and the team at Eye Books for helping drag what is written here out of me. I am also immeasurably grateful to my family – Camilla, Will, Rose and Theo – for their patience as I have tested ideas on them. They kindly read innumerable drafts and let me know when they thought I was hitting the mark and when it was obvious to everyone but me that I was losing the plot. I can also never thank them enough for all their constant love and support over many years when I was absent and distracted by a multi-decade mission to collect the raw material needed to write this book.